A
CATULLUS
Workbook

LLWS

Latin Literature Workbook Series

A Series Edited by LeaAnn A. Osburn

A CATULLUS Workbook

Helena Dettmer
& LeaAnn A. Osburn

With a Glossary by
Ronnie Ancona

Bolchazy-Carducci Publishers, Inc.
Mundelein, Illinois USA

Series Editor
LeaAnn A. Osburn

Volume General Editor
Donald E. Sprague

Typography, Page and Cover Design
Adam Phillip Velez

A Catullus Workbook

by Helena Dettmer & LeaAnn A. Osburn

© 2006 Bolchazy-Carducci Publishers, Inc.
All rights reserved.

Bolchazy-Carducci Publishers, Inc.
1570 Baskin Road
Mundelein, IL 60060 USA
www.bolchazy.com

Printed in the United States of America
2009
by United Graphics

ISBN 978-0-86516-623-3

The glossary of the present work appeared
in a slightly different version
in *Writing Passion: A Catullus Reader*, by Ronnie Ancona
Bolchazy-Carducci Publishers (2004): 221–263.
©2004 by Bolchazy-Carducci Publishers.

CONTENTS

FOREWORD

All Latin teachers want their students to read ancient authors in the original. Yet to study the authentic Latin of an ancient Roman author is a complex task. It requires comprehension of the text and its grammatical underpinnings; an understanding of the world events and the culture in which the work of literature was produced; an ability to recognize the figures of speech the author uses and to grasp the impact they have on the text; sensitivity to the way sound effects, including meter if a passage is poetry, interact with the meaning of the text; and the ability to probe whatever thoughts and ideas the author may be expressing. To be successful in this multifaceted task, students need not only a comprehensive textbook but also exercises of different kinds, in which to practice their newly developing literary and critical skills.

Students often need extensive drill and practice material—something not available in the traditional Latin author textbook—to help them master the grammar and syntax of the Latin text as well as the literary skills that the text demands of its readers. Teachers, too, no matter how many questions they ask in class to help their students analyze the syntax and the literary qualities of the text, often need and want more questions to be available. Realizing this need on the part of both students and teachers, Bolchazy-Carducci Publishers has begun to develop a series of workbooks to accompany Advanced Placement textbooks. There will be five workbooks in the series, one for each advanced placement author: Catullus, Cicero, Horace, Ovid, and Vergil. A team of authors—one, a university scholar with special expertise in the Latin literary text and the other, a high school Advanced Placement Latin teacher—will write each workbook.

Workbooks in this series will contain the Latin text as delineated on the Advanced Placement Syllabus and exercises that drill grammar, syntax, and figures of speech. In addition, multiple choice questions will be included and will focus on the student's comprehension of the passage and on items of literary analysis. The workbooks will also feature scansion practice, essays to write, and other short analysis questions in each section. By reading and answering these types of questions, students will gain experience with the types of questions that are found on the Advanced Placement Examinations. Students at the college level will also benefit from the additional practice offered in the workbooks.

These workbooks contain neither textual notes nor vocabulary on the page with the text nor on the facing page. The absence of these traditional features of textbooks will allow students, after reading the Latin passage in the textbook, to practice in the workbook what they have learned and to assess how much they have mastered already and what needs more study. The workbooks will, however, contain a Latin to English Vocabulary at the back of the book.

We are confident that this series of workbooks has a unique role to play in fostering students' understanding of authentic Latin text and will be a significant addition to the Advanced Placement and college materials that already exist.

LeaAnn A. Osburn
Series Editor

PREFACE

It has been a pleasure for both of us to write this workbook that has been designed to aid students who are reading the poetry of Catullus for the first time. This workbook is intended for students preparing for the Advanced Placement Examination and for college students reading the poems of Catullus as part of their course work. Because we are writing for this dual audience, the text of each Catullan poem is followed by a variety of exercises. All of the various exercises are intended to help students at both the high school or college level understand and interpret the poems, and they should be assigned or used in whatever way best assists the students in this process. In the discussion to follow, however, the comments about the exercises are directed primarily at the students and teachers who are preparing for the AP* Latin Literature Examination.

I. Short Answer Questions

These questions, which follow the poem line by line, deal largely with grammar, syntax, and vocabulary. Although these questions are not of the type featured on any of the AP* Latin Examinations, we believe that if students answer them, they will be better prepared to understand each line of the poem. These short answer questions may be done at sight in class before the poem is assigned as homework, thereby functioning as a pre-reading exercise, or they may be answered as the student reads each line of the poem. In fact, the questions may be used in whatever way the teacher or student wishes.

II. Multiple Choice Questions

On Part I of the Advanced Placement Latin Literature Examination, multiple choice questions follow three unseen passages and one seen passage from the AP* Catullus syllabus. As a result, the multiple choice questions in this workbook will be especially useful to those preparing for the examination. These questions concern comprehension, grammar, syntax, references, figures of speech, and interpretation. Questions about translation and metrics are not found as often in this section, as they are on the AP* Examinations, since separate exercises are included that pertain to these items.

III. Translation

Passages chosen for translation are generally of medium difficulty. It should be noted that sometimes the length of the passage is shorter than what is found on the AP* Examination but the teacher may still use an AP-type rubric when grading the translation. Whereas on the Advanced Placement Examination translating the passage requires that students confront a passage that they may not have seen recently, the design of this workbook gives students practice with translation shortly after they have

---

*   AP is a registered trademark of the College Entrance Examination Board, which was not involved in the production of, and does not endorse, this product.

read the assigned poem. The translation section offers several possibilities. By writing out the translation after a recent reading of the poem, students will gain practice in writing a literal translation that follows the Latin closely in respect to tense, voice, mood, number, person, and cases. Alternatively, the teacher may choose to omit the translation exercise until another five or six poems have been read. By assigning the omitted translation at a later date, the experience of the Advanced Placement Examination can be mimicked in the classroom. Others may wish not to assign the translation exercise until the entire Catullus syllabus is completed and then use the translation exercises as a way to start a review of each poem.

IV. Short and Long Essay Questions

Both the short and long essay questions are intended for use after the poem has been read in its entirety and discussed in class.

Short essay questions focus on certain aspects of the poem without usually requiring that the student address the entire poem. The suggested time allotment for these questions is twenty minutes. Teachers may choose to impose or ignore the time limit, depending on the needs of the class. The time allotment, at the very least, indicates to students how much time they should plan on using for the short essay question when they write the AP* Examination. Sometimes students are given a choice between two or three short essay questions. Teachers may instruct students to write an answer for all the questions or may assign just one for all students to do and thereby save the other questions as a source for classroom discussion.

Long essay questions have a time allotment of thirty minutes, which the teacher may enforce or not. They may be given in class in order that students have an experience that is as close as possible to the one that they will have on the AP* Examination. Long essay questions also may become an out-of-class assignment or may be used as a topic for classroom discussion.

In both short and long essay questions, students are asked to cite and translate the Latin from the poem to support the points in the essay. This standard way to write an essay that involves literary analysis is critical to success on the AP* Examination. Students need to focus on analyzing the poetry in depth rather than simply describing its content.

Some poems offer both a short and a long essay question, while other poems offer either one or the other.

V. Scansion

The meters required by the AP* Examination for the Catullus examination are the hendecasyllabic, dactylic hexameter, Sapphic stanza, and elegiac couplet. Some of Catullus' poems are in other meters. Because meter can enhance the meaning of a poem, a scansion exercise concludes the set of exercises for each poem.

*　*　*　*　*　*　*　*

---

* AP is a registered trademark of the College Entrance Examination Board, which was not involved in the production of, and does not endorse, this product.

We followed the Oxford text in preparing this workbook but changed consonantal u's to v's. The text of our workbook also differs from the Oxford text in a few minor points of punctuation and in the following readings:

in Poem 14, line 16, we read *salse* for *false*;

in Poem 65, lines 2 and 15, we read *Hortalus* for *Ortalus*;

in Poem 68, lines 11 and 30, we read *Manli* for *Mani*;

in Poem 116, line 7, we read *acta* for †*amitha*.

No macrons appear in this workbook (except in the glossary) just as macrons are not used on the AP* Examinations. The term "figure of speech," as used in this workbook, refers to a group of terms used in literary analysis such as figures of thought, tropes, literary devices, and rhetorical figures of speech. Those figures of speech that are required by the Advanced Placement syllabus can be found in the "Acorn" book or at the AP* website, www.apcentral.org. This workbook does not limit itself only to the AP* required figures of speech because we believe that other devices can often allow students to see the poetry of Catullus from a different angle and thus enhance their appreciation of the poetry. The figure of speech that is sometimes called interlocked word order is identified in this workbook by the more formal term "synchysis," which is also spelled "synchesis" in some texts. "Tricolon crescens," sometimes written as "tricolon crescendo" in other texts, is the term used in this workbook.

We would like to offer our sincere thanks to Bolchazy-Carducci Publishers for offering us this opportunity. In addition, we would like to acknowledge the work of several people who have contributed significantly to this project: our editor, Donald E. Sprague, Ronnie Ancona, the two Bolchazy-Carducci peer readers, and all of our students who have permitted us to realize anew what a joy it is to read the poetry of Catullus for the first time.

HELENA DETTMER
University of Iowa

LEAANN A. OSBURN
Barrington High School, retired

TEXT OF
THE *POEMS*
WITH EXERCISES

CATULLUS 1

Cui dono lepidum novum libellum
arida modo pumice expolitum?
Corneli, tibi: namque tu solebas
meas esse aliquid putare nugas
5   iam tum, cum ausus es unus Italorum
omne aevum tribus explicare cartis
doctis, Iuppiter, et laboriosis.
quare habe tibi quidquid hoc libelli
qualecumque; quod, <o> patrona virgo,
10   plus uno maneat perenne saeclo.

Short Answer Questions

Line 1   What is the case and use of *cui?* _____

           Which word is a diminutive? _____

Line 2   What case is *expolitum* and why? _____

Line 3   What case is *Corneli?* _____

Line 4   What is the use of the infinitive *putare?* _____

Line 5   Translate *ausus es.* _____

Line 7   What word does *laboriosis* modify? _____

Line 8   What is the case and use of *libelli?* _____

Line 9   What is the antecedent of *quod?* _____

Line 10 What is the mood and use of *maneat?* _____

           What is the case and use of *saeclo?* _____

Multiple Choice Questions *Suggested time: 11 minutes*

1. In line 1, the subject of *dono* refers to
    a. Cornelius
    b. Jupiter
    c. a girl
    d. Catullus

2. In line 2, *pumice* is modified by
    a. *cui* (line 1)
    b. *novum* (line 1)
    c. *arida* (line 2)
    d. *modo* (line 2)

3. From lines 1–4, we learn that
    a. Cornelius is writing a new type of book
    b. Cornelius will be sent a new type of book
    c. Cornelius believes the new book is not worthwhile
    d. Cornelius thinks the new book is too small

4. In line 4, the subject of *esse* is
    a. *tu* (line 3)
    b. *nugas* (line 4)
    c. *unus* (line 5)
    d. *aevum* (line 6)

5. The infinitive *explicare* (line 6) is complementary to
    a. *ausus es* (line 5)
    b. *cartis* (line 6)
    c. *doctis* (line 7)
    d. *habe* (line 8)

6. In lines 5–7, Cornelius' writing is described as
    a. a history in three volumes
    b. a story about one Italian
    c. a book that teaches about Jupiter
    d. a tale of daring labors

7. In line 7, there is an example of
    a. chiasmus
    b. an oxymoron
    c. metonymy
    d. apostrophe

8. In line 9, to whom does the *virgo* refer?
    a. Catullus' girlfriend
    b. Cornelius' daughter
    c. a muse
    d. one of Jupiter's lovers

9. The subject of *maneat* (line 10) is
    a   *quod* (line 9)
    b. *virgo* (line 9)
    c. *patrona* (line 9)
    d. *saeclo* (line 10)

Translation *Suggested time: 10 minutes*

Translate the passage below as literally as possible.

> **Corneli, tibi: namque tu solebas**
> **meas esse aliquid putare nugas**
> **iam tum, cum ausus es unus Italorum**
> **omne aevum tribus explicare cartis**
> 5   **doctis, Iuppiter, et laboriosis.**

_____

_____

_____

_____

_____

_____

_____

Short Essay *Suggested time: 20 minutes*

Give two different meanings for the word *expolitum* in line 2 and explain how this word plays a key role in the thought of the entire poem.

Support your assertions with references drawn from **throughout** the poem. All Latin words must be copied or their line numbers provided, AND they must be translated or paraphrased closely enough so that it is clear you understand the Latin. It is your responsibility to convince your reader that you are basing your conclusions on the Latin text and not merely on a general recollection of the passage. Direct your answer to the question; do not merely summarize the passage. Please write your essay on a separate piece of paper.

Long Essay *Suggested time: 30 minutes*

Discuss what Catullus considers to be good poetry, according to the information presented in Poem 1.

Support your assertions with references drawn from **throughout** the poem. All Latin words must be copied or their line numbers provided, AND they must be translated or paraphrased closely enough so that it is clear you understand the Latin. It is your responsibility to convince your reader that you are basing your conclusions on the Latin text and not merely on a general recollection of the passage. Direct your answer to the question; do not merely summarize the passage. Please write your essay on a separate piece of paper.

Scansion

Scan the following lines and name the meter.

iam tum, cum ausus es unus Italorum

omne aevum tribus explicare cartis

doctis, Iuppiter, et laboriosis.

CATULLUS 2

Passer, deliciae meae puellae,
quicum ludere, quem in sinu tenere,
cui primum digitum dare appetenti
et acris solet incitare morsus,
5   cum desiderio meo nitenti
carum nescio quid lubet iocari,
et solaciolum sui doloris,
credo, ut tum gravis acquiescat ardor:
tecum ludere sicut ipsa possem
10   et tristis animi levare curas!

Short Answer Questions

Line 1   What word is in apposition with *passer*? _____

Line 2   What verb does *ludere* complement? _____

Line 3   What case is *appetenti,* and what word does it modify? _____

Line 4   What is the equivalent prose form of *acris?* _____

Line 5   What is the meaning of *cum* in the context of this sentence? _____

Line 7   What word does *sui* modify? _____

Line 8   What is the mood, tense, and voice of *acquiescat?* _____

Line 9   What is the mood and use of *possem?* _____

Line 10   What case is *tristis,* and what word does it modify?_____

Multiple Choice Questions *Suggested time: 10 minutes*

1.   The antecedent of *cui* (line 3) is

   a. *passer* (line 1)   b. *puellae* (line 1)
   c. *sinu* (line 2)   d. *digitum* (line 3)

2.   In line 4, *et acris solet incitare morsus* is translated

   a. and is accustomed to sharply bite and   b. and is accustomed to incite sharp bites
       incite
   c. and the sharpness is accustomed to   d. and the bite is accustomed to being sharp
       incite bites

3. From lines 1–4, we learn that

   a. the girlfriend is biting her fingertip

                                     b. the girlfriend cannot get the sparrow to sit in her lap

   c. the girlfriend does not like the sparrow

                                     d. the girlfriend is playing with the sparrow

4. According to line 7, *dolor* is being felt by

   a. the sparrow   b. the girl

   c. Catullus   d. you

5. In line 8, the verb *acquiescat* is in a(n)

   a. indirect statement   b. clause of fearing

   c. purpose clause   d. indirect command

6. In line 8, which of these can be found?

   a. a diminutive   b. two dactyls

   c. an elision   d. an apostrophe

7. In lines 5–8, it is disclosed that

   a. the girl is the object of Catullus' love

                                      b. Catullus does not know how to joke with the girl

   c. the sparrow is in pain

                                      d. the flames of a fire can be seen shining

8. In line 9, to whom does *ipsa* refer?

   a. the sparrow   b. the girl

   c. Catullus' desire   d. the girl's passion

Translation *Suggested time: 4 minutes*

Translate the passage below as literally as possible.

> **tecum ludere sicut ipsa possem**
> **et tristis animi levare curas!**

_____

_____

_____

_____

Short Essay *Suggested time: 20 minutes*

Catullus uses the language of love in Poem 2 to describe Lesbia's affection for the *passer*. Give examples of this language and discuss how it contributes to the meaning of the poem.

Support your assertions with references drawn from **throughout** the poem. All Latin words must be copied or their line numbers provided, AND they must be translated or paraphrased closely enough so that it is clear you understand the Latin. It is your responsibility to convince your reader that you are basing your conclusions on the Latin text and not merely on a general recollection of the passage. Direct your answer to the question; do not merely summarize the passage. Please write your essay on a separate piece of paper.

Scansion

Scan the following lines and name the meter.

Passer, deliciae meae puellae,

quicum ludere, quem in sinu tenere,

CATULLUS 3

Lugete, o Veneres Cupidinesque,
et quantum est hominum venustiorum:
passer mortuus est meae puellae,
passer, deliciae meae puellae,
5   quem plus illa oculis suis amabat.
nam mellitus erat suamque norat
ipsam tam bene quam puella matrem,
nec sese a gremio illius movebat,
sed circumsiliens modo huc modo illuc
10   ad solam dominam usque pipiabat;
qui nunc it per iter tenebricosum
illud, unde negant redire quemquam.
at vobis male sit, malae tenebrae
Orci, quae omnia bella devoratis:
15   tam bellum mihi passerem abstulistis.
o factum male! o miselle passer!
tua nunc opera meae puellae
flendo turgiduli rubent ocelli.

Short Answer Questions

Line 1   What grammatical form is *lugete?* _____

Line 2   What is the case and use of *hominum?* _____

Line 5   What is the antecedent of *quem?* _____

               What is the case and use of *oculis?* _____

Line 6   What is the unsyncopated form of *norat?* _____

Line 8   What is the case and use of *gremio?*_____

Line 9   Translate *circumsiliens.* _____

Line 11   What word does *tenebricosum* modify? _____

Line 13   What is the mood and use of *sit?*_____

Line 15   What is the case and use of *mihi?* _____

Line 16   What is the case and use of *passer?* _____

Line 17   What is the case and use of *opera?* _____

Line 18   What is the grammatical form and case of *flendo?* _____

Multiple Choice Questions *Suggested time: 13 minutes*

1. In lines 3–4, there is an example of

    a. chiasmus   b. zeugma

    c. anaphora   d. allegory

2. In line 5, *quem plus illa oculis suis amabat* is translated

    a. for whom it was a plus that she loved with her eyes
    b. whom she loved more than her own eyes

    c. whom he loved more than her with his own eyes
    d. in whose eyes she was loved more than could be said

3. To whom does *illa* (line 5) refer?

    a. the sparrow   b. the girl

    c. the girl's mother   d. Venus

4. From lines 1–5, we learn that

    a. Venus and Cupid are mourning the death of the girl
    b. charming men are mourning the absence of Venus and Cupid

    c. the girl wants to see the sparrow with her own eyes
    d. the sparrow is dead

5. In line 8, *illius* refers to

    a. the girl   b. Catullus

    c. the sparrow   d. Venus

6. The actions described in lines 6–10 are those of

    a. Catullus   b. the sparrow

    c. the girl   d. Cupid

7. In line 12, *unde negant redire quemquam* is translated

    a. the waves deny anyone from going back
    b. where anyone can go back

    c. from where they say no one returns
    d. who deny returning also

8. The antecedent of *quae* (line 14) is

    a. *quemquam* (line 12)   b. *tenebrae* (line 13)

    c. *Orci* (line 14)   d. *bella* (line 14)

9. In lines 11–15,

    a. the sparrow is denied entrance to Orcus
    b. Orcus steals away the sparrow

    c. the sparrow eats everything in sight
    d. the shadows of Orcus make war

10. Line 16 contains

    a. an anastrophe

    b. a diminutive

    c. a nominative

    d. an aposiopesis

11. In line 18, the subject of *rubent* is

    a. *opera* (line 17)

    b. *puellae* (line 17)

    c. *flendo* (line 18)

    d. *ocelli* (line 18)

Translation *Suggested time: 6 minutes*

Translate the passage below as literally as possible.

> **nec sese a gremio illius movebat,**
> **sed circumsiliens modo huc modo illuc**
> **ad solam dominam usque pipiabat;**

_____

_____

_____

_____

_____

Long Essay *Suggested time: 30 minutes*

Poem 3 is notable for its many elisions. Cite at least four examples of elision and discuss how they contribute to the meaning of the poem.

Support your assertions with references drawn from **throughout** the poem. All Latin words must be copied or their line numbers provided, AND they must be translated or paraphrased closely enough so that it is clear you understand the Latin. It is your responsibility to convince your reader that you are basing your conclusions on the Latin text and not merely on a general recollection of the passage. Direct your answer to the question; do not merely summarize the passage. Please write your essay on a separate piece of paper.

Scansion

Scan the following lines and name the meter.

> nec sese a gremio illius movebat,
>
> sed circumsiliens modo huc modo illuc
>
> ad solam dominam usque pipiabat;

CATULLUS 4

Phaselus ille, quem videtis, hospites,
ait fuisse navium celerrimus,
neque ullius natantis impetum trabis
nequisse praeterire, sive palmulis
5   opus foret volare sive linteo.
et hoc negat minacis Hadriatici
negare litus insulasve Cycladas
Rhodumque nobilem horridamque Thraciam
Propontida trucemve Ponticum sinum,
10 ubi iste post phaselus antea fuit
comata silva; nam Cytorio in iugo
loquente saepe sibilum edidit coma.
Amastri Pontica et Cytore buxifer,
tibi haec fuisse et esse cognitissima
15 ait phaselus: ultima ex origine
tuo stetisse dicit in cacumine,
tuo imbuisse palmulas in aequore,
et inde tot per impotentia freta
erum tulisse, laeva sive dextera
20 vocaret aura, sive utrumque Iuppiter
simul secundus incidisset in pedem;
neque ulla vota litoralibus deis
sibi esse facta, cum veniret a mari
novissimo hunc ad usque limpidum lacum.
25 sed haec prius fuere: nunc recondita
senet quiete seque dedicat tibi,
gemelle Castor et gemelle Castoris.

Short Answer Questions

Line 1   What case is *hospites?* _____

Line 2   What is the tense and form of *fuisse?* _____

Line 3   What case and number is *ullius?* _____

Line 4   What is the case and use of *palmulis?* _____

Line 5   What is the alternate form of *foret?* _____

          Translate *opus foret.* _____

Line 7   What is the case and use of *litus?* _____

Line 9   What is the meaning of *trucem,* and what word does it modify? _____

Line 10   What part of speech is *post?* _____

Line 12   What is the case and use of *coma?* _____

Line 13   What is the case and use of *Cytore?* _____

Line 14   What is the case, use, and form of *cognitissima?* _____

Line 16   What is the grammatical form of *stetisse?* _____

Line 17   What word modifies *aequore?* _____

Line 19   Translate *erum.* _____

Line 20   Why is *vocaret* in the subjunctive? _____

Line 21   What is the mood and tense of *incidisset?* _____

              What word modifies *Iuppiter?* _____

Line 22   What is the case and use of *litoralibus deis?* _____

Line 23   In what type of clause is the verb *veniret?* _____

Line 25   What is the unsyncopated form of *fuere?* _____

              What word does *recondita* modify? _____

Line 27   What is the case and use of *gemelle?* _____

Multiple Choice Questions *Suggested time: 15 minutes*

1.   What is the antecedent of *quem* (line 1)?
     a. *phaselus* (line 1)   b. *hospites* (line 1)
     c. *trabis* (line 3)   d. *impetum* (line 3)

2.   In line 2, what is *celerrimus* modifying?
     a. *phaselus* (line 1)   b. *trabis* (line 3)
     c. *palmulis* (line 4)   d. *linteo* (line 5)

3.   In lines 1–5
     a. the boat indicates that Catullus' guests   b. the boat claims that it is faster than other
         travelled on it   boats
     c. the boat says that it can swim because   d. the boat states that it does not have any
         of its beams   sails

4. In line 8, there is an example of

   a. chiasmus
   b. synecdoche
   c. anastrophe
   d. litotes

5. In line 10, *iste* refers to

   a. *phaselus* (line 10)
   b. *silva* (line 11)
   c. *iugo* (line 11)
   d. *coma* (line 12)

6. The best translation of line 12 is

   a. it often brought forth a rustle from its speaking foliage
   b. it often ate, rustled, and spoke with its foliage
   c. it often spoke about its rustling foliage
   d. it often rustled about its foliage and speech

7. From lines 6–12, we learn

   a. how forests fill several places that are mentioned in these lines
   b. of several places to which the boat travelled
   c. that the boat denies that it ever went to the Cyclades islands
   d. why the Adriatic Sea threatened the boat

8. In line 16, *cacumine* refers to

   a. *Amastri* (line 13)
   b. *Cytore* (line 13)
   c. *Thraciam* (line 8)
   d. *Rhodum* (line 8)

9. In line 20, *Iuppiter* by metonymy means

   a. wind
   b. lightning
   c. king
   d. lover

10. Lines 13–21 reveal

    a. that the boat had once been a tree on a mountain top
    b. that the boat's oars had broken apart because of the weather on the sea
    c. that Jupiter had fallen over his foot
    d. that the master had not navigated the boat very well, either on the left or on the right

11. In line 23, *sibi* refers to

    a. *phaselus* (line 15)
    b. *Iuppiter* (line 20)
    c. *mari* (line 23)
    d. *lacum* (line 24)

12. From lines 22–27, we learn that

    a. just now the boat has come from the sea to the lake
    b. the boat made vows to the shore gods
    c. Castor and his twin dedicate themselves to the boat
    d. there is no quiet for the boat in a secluded place

13. What figure of speech dominates Poem 4?

    a. assonance

    b. aposiopesis

    c. personification

    d. antithesis

Translation *Suggested time: 5 minutes*

Translate the passage below as literally as possible.

> **Amastri Pontica et Cytore buxifer,**
> **tibi haec fuisse et esse cognitissima**
> **ait phaselus:**

_____

_____

_____

_____

Short Essay *Suggested time: 20 minutes*

Find at least three examples of alliteration in Poem 4 and discuss how they enhance the meaning of the poem.

Support your assertions with references drawn from **throughout** the poem. All Latin words must be copied or their line numbers provided, AND they must be translated or paraphrased closely enough so that it is clear you understand the Latin. It is your responsibility to convince your reader that you are basing your conclusions on the Latin text and not merely on a general recollection of the passage. Direct your answer to the question; do not merely summarize the passage. Please write your essay on a separate piece of paper.

Long Essay *Suggested time: 30 minutes*

Discuss how the life of the boat as described by Catullus reflects the human experience.

Support your assertions with references drawn from **throughout** the poem. All Latin words must be copied or their line numbers provided, AND they must be translated or paraphrased closely enough so that it is clear you understand the Latin. It is your responsibility to convince your reader that you are basing your conclusions on the Latin text and not merely on a general recollection of the passage. Direct your answer to the question; do not merely summarize the passage. Please write your essay on a separate piece of paper.

Scansion

Scan the following lines and identify the non-AP meter.

Rhodumque nobilem horridamque Thraciam

Propontida trucemve Ponticum sinum,

ubi iste post phaselus antea fuit

CATULLUS 5

Vivamus, mea Lesbia, atque amemus,
rumoresque senum severiorum
omnes unius aestimemus assis!
soles occidere et redire possunt:
5   nobis, cum semel occidit brevis lux,
nox est perpetua una dormienda.
da mi basia mille, deinde centum,
dein mille altera, dein secunda centum,
deinde usque altera mille, deinde centum.
10   dein, cum milia multa fecerimus,
conturbabimus illa, ne sciamus,
aut ne quis malus invidere possit,
cum tantum sciat esse basiorum.

Short Answer Questions

Line 1   What is the mood and use of *vivamus?* _____

Line 2   Translate *senum severiorum.* _____

Line 3   What case and use is *assis?* _____

Line 5   What is the case and use of *nobis?* _____

             What type of clause does *cum* introduce? _____

Line 6   What construction is *est . . . dormienda?* _____

Line 7   *Mi* is the shortened form of what Latin word? _____

Line 9   To what word does *altera* refer? _____

Line 10   What mood and tense is *fecerimus?* _____

Line 11   What is the mood, tense, and use of *sciamus?* _____

Line 13   What case and use is *tantum?* _____

Multiple Choice Questions *Suggested time: 6 minutes*

1. The subject of *amemus* (line 1) refers to
    a. the old men
    c. Lesbia and her lovers

    b. Lesbia and Catullus
    d. all Romans

2. In line 2, it is implied that the rumors are about
    a. a coin named an *as* that is owed
    c. the love of Lesbia and Catullus

    b. strictness of the old men
    d. when the sun will set

3. In line 5, *brevis lux* refers to
    a. life
    c. the gossip of the old men

    b. lamp light
    d. the sunrise

4. In lines 7–10, there is example of
    a. anaphora
    c. irony

    b. hysteron proteron
    d. metaphor

5. *milia multa* (line 10) refers to
    a. *soles* (line 4)
    c. *nox* (line 6)

    b. *lux* (line 5)
    d. *basia* (line 7)

Translation *Suggested time: 5 minutes*

Translate the passage below as literally as possible.

> **nobis, cum semel occidit brevis lux,**
> **nox est perpetua una dormienda.**

_____

_____

_____

_____

Short Essay *Suggested time: 20 minutes*

Discuss how the juxtaposition of *lux* and *nox* enhances lines 5–6 and plays a role in the thought of the poem.

Support your assertions with references drawn from the poem. All Latin words must be copied or their line numbers provided, AND they must be translated or paraphrased closely enough so that it is clear you understand the Latin. It is your responsibility to convince your reader that you are basing your conclusions on the Latin text and not merely on a general recollection of the passage. Direct your answer to the question; do not merely summarize the passage. Please write your essay on a separate piece of paper.

Scansion

Scan the following lines and name the meter.

deinde usque altera mille, deinde centum;

dein, cum milia multa fecerimus,

conturbabimus illa, ne sciamus,

CATULLUS 7

Quaeris, quot mihi basiationes
tuae, Lesbia, sint satis superque.
quam magnus numerus Libyssae harenae
lasarpiciferis iacet Cyrenis
5   oraclum Iovis inter aestuosi
et Batti veteris sacrum sepulcrum;
aut quam sidera multa, cum tacet nox,
furtivos hominum vident amores:
tam te basia multa basiare
10   vesano satis et super Catullo est,
quae nec pernumerare curiosi
possint nec mala fascinare lingua.

Short Answer Questions

Line 2   What is the mood and use of *sint?* _____

               What case is Lesbia? _____

Line 4   What is the subject of *iacet?* _____

               What is the case and use of *Cyrenis?* _____

Line 5   What word does *aestuosi* modify? _____

Line 6   What is the case and use of *sepulcrum?*_____

Line 9   What is the case and use of *basia multa?* _____

Line 10   What is the subject of *est*? _____

Line 12   What is the tense, mood, and use of *possint?* _____

               What is the case and use of *lingua*? _____

Multiple Choice Questions *Suggested time: 6 minutes*

1. Lines 1–2
   a. contain two examples of alliteration
   b. are an elegiac couplet
   c. contain one elision
   d. are an example of asyndeton

2. According to lines 3–7, the answer to the question posed in line 1
   a. can be seen in silphium-bearing Cyrene near the oracle
   b. will be given by old Battus near his holy tomb
   c. is the number of grains of desert sand and stars in the sky
   d. will be revealed when night in its silence arrives

3. In line 8, the subject of *vident* is
   a. Jupiter and Battus
   b. the loves
   c. the night
   d. the stars

4. The antecedent of *quae* (line 11) is
   a. *basia* (line 9)
   b. *Catullo* (line 10)
   c. *curiosi* (line 11)
   d. *lingua* (line 12)

5. In lines 10–12, there is an example of a(n)
   a. diminutive
   b. apostrophe
   c. elision
   d. oxymoron

Translation *Suggested time: 4 minutes*

Translate the passage below as literally as possible.

> aut quam sidera multa, cum tacet nox,
> furtivos hominum vident amores:

_____

_____

_____

_____

Long Essay *Suggested time: 30 minutes*

Vivamus, mea Lesbia, atque amemus,
rumoresque senum severiorum
omnes unius aestimemus assis!
soles occidere et redire possunt;
5 nobis, cum semel occidit brevis lux,
nox est perpetua una dormienda.
da mi basia mille, deinde centum,
dein mille altera, dein secunda centum,
deinde usque altera mille, dende centum.
10 dein, cum milia multa fecerimus,
conturbabimus illa, ne sciamus
aut ne quis malus invidere possit,
cum tantum sciat esse basiorum.

Catullus 5

Quaeris, quot mihi basiationes
tuae, Lesbia, sint satis superque.
quam magnus numerus Libyssae harenae
lasarpiciferis iacet Cyrenis
5 oraclum Iovis inter aestuosi
et Batti veteris sacrum sepulcrum;
aut quam sidera multa, cum tacet nox,
furtivos hominum vident amores:
tam te basia multa basiare
10 vesano satis et super Catullo est,
quae nec pernumerare curiosi
possint nec mala fascinare lingua.

Catullus 7

Discuss how the content, diction, and structure of Poem 7 establish its thematic connection to Poem 5.

Support your assertions with references drawn from **throughout** both poems. All Latin words must be copied or their line numbers provided, AND they must be translated or paraphrased closely enough so that it is clear you understand the Latin. It is your responsibility to convince your reader that you are basing your conclusions on the Latin text and not merely on a general recollection of the passage. Direct your answer to the question; do not merely summarize the passage. Please write your essay on a separate piece of paper.

Scansion

Scan the following lines and name the meter.

vesano satis et super Catullo est,

quae nec pernumerare curiosi

possint nec mala fascinare lingua.

CATULLUS 8

Miser Catulle, desinas ineptire,
et quod vides perisse perditum ducas.
fulsere quondam candidi tibi soles,
cum ventitabas quo puella ducebat
5   amata nobis quantum amabitur nulla.
ibi illa multa cum iocosa fiebant,
quae tu volebas nec puella nolebat,
fulsere vere candidi tibi soles.
nunc iam illa non volt: tu quoque inpote<ns noli>,
10   nec quae fugit sectare, nec miser vive,
sed obstinata mente perfer, obdura.
vale, puella. iam Catullus obdurat,
nec te requiret nec rogabit invitam.
at tu dolebis, cum rogaberis nulla.
15   scelesta, vae te, quae tibi manet vita?
quis nunc te adibit? cui videberis bella?
quem nunc amabis? cuius esse diceris?
quem basiabis? cui labella mordebis?
at tu, Catulle, destinatus obdura.

Short Answer Questions

Line 1   What word does *miser* modify? _____

                  What is the mood and use of *desinas*? _____

Line 2   What is the tense and voice of *perisse*? _____

Line 3   What is the alternate form of *fulsere*? _____

Line 4   Translate *quo*._____

Line 5   What is the case and use of *nobis*? _____

Line 6   What part of speech is *cum*? _____

Line 8   What word does *candidi* modify?_____

Line 10   What is the mood and voice of *sectare*? _____

Line 11   What word does *obstinata* modify? _____

Line 15   What case is *te* and why? _____

Line 17   Translate *cuius*. _____

                 What is the tense, mood, and voice of *diceris*? _____

Line 18   What is the case and use of *labella*? _____

Multiple Choice Questions *Suggested time: 13 minutes*

1. From lines 1–2, it is clear that
    a. Catullus thinks the girl is acting silly
    b. Catullus has lost something
    c. Catullus is leading the girl around
    d. Catullus is looking at the girl

2. In line 3, *tibi* refers to
    a. the girl
    b. Lesbia
    c. Catullus
    d. the reader

3. The form of the word *ventitabas* (line 4) emphasizes
    a. the frequency of the action
    b. the completed nature of the action
    c. the current state of the action
    d. the uncertainty of the action

4. In line 5, *nobis* refers to
    a. Lesbia's new lovers
    b. the girl
    c. Catullus
    d. Catullus and his new girlfriend

5. Line 7 contains an example of
    a. litotes
    b. polysyndeton
    c. hypallage
    d. ecphrasis

6. In lines 3 and 8, the *candidi soles* refer to
    a. the good weather when Catullus was with the girl
    b. the time of day when Catullus was with the girl
    c. the good times Catullus and the girl used to have
    d. the lonely feelings Catullus had when he was not with the girl

7. In line 10, *quae* refers to
    a. Catullus
    b. the girl
    c. the love they felt
    d. their enjoyment

8. Line 11 contains an example of
    a. pleonasm
    b. tmesis
    c. synchysis
    d. prolepsis

9. In line 12, *vale, puella* is an example of

   a. ellipsis

   b. zeugma

   c. synizesis

   d. apostrophe

10. In lines 9–13, we learn that

    a. Catullus is in despair over the loss of his love

    b. Catullus decides to break up with the girl

    c. Catullus thinks the girl will live miserably without him

    d. Catullus feels the girl is being obstinate

11. The series of rhetorical questions in lines 15–18

    a. is designed to ease the torment the girl is feeling

    b. indicates to the girl what she will be missing

    c. shows how agitated the girl is

    d. points out the fidelity that the girl has shown to Catullus

Translate *Suggested time: 4 minutes*

Translate the passage below as literally as possible.

> **vale, puella. iam Catullus obdurat,**
> **nec te requiret nec rogabit invitam.**

_____

_____

_____

_____

Short Essay *Suggested time: 20 minutes*

The verb *obduro* occurs in lines 11, 12, and 19. How does the repetition of this word sum up the thought of Poem 8?

Support your assertions with references drawn from **throughout** the poem. All Latin words must be copied or their line numbers provided, AND they must be translated or paraphrased closely enough so that it is clear you understand the Latin. It is your responsibility to convince your reader that you are basing your conclusions on the Latin text and not merely on a general recollection of the passage. Direct your answer to the question; do not merely summarize the passage. Please write your essay on a separate piece of paper.

Long Essay *Suggested time: 30 minutes*

Discuss how the dramatic character of the poem is enhanced by Catullus' addressing himself.

Support your assertions with references drawn from **throughout** the poem. All Latin words must be copied or their line numbers provided, AND they must be translated or paraphrased closely enough so that it is clear you understand the Latin. It is your responsibility to convince your reader that you are basing your conclusions on the Latin text and not merely on a general recollection of the passage. Direct your answer to the question; do not merely summarize the passage. Please write your essay on a separate piece of paper.

Scansion

Scan the following lines and identify the non-AP meter.

nunc iam illa non volt: tu quoque inpote<ns noli>,

nec quae fugit sectare, nec miser vive,

sed obstinata mente prefer, obdura.

CATULLUS 10

Varus me meus ad suos amores
visum duxerat e foro otiosum,
scortillum, ut mihi tum repente visum est,
non sane illepidum neque invenustum.
5 huc ut venimus, incidere nobis
sermones varii, in quibus, quid esset
iam Bithynia, quo modo se haberet,
et quonam mihi profuisset aere.
respondi id quod erat, nihil neque ipsis
10 nec praetoribus esse nec cohorti,
cur quisquam caput unctius referret,
praesertim quibus esset irrumator
praetor, nec faceret pili cohortem.
"at certe tamen," inquiunt "quod illic
15 natum dicitur esse, comparasti
ad lecticam homines." ego, ut puellae
unum me facerem beatiorem,
"non" inquam "mihi tam fuit maligne,
ut, provincia quod mala incidisset,
20 non possem octo homines parare rectos."
at mi nullus erat nec hic neque illic,
fractum qui veteris pedem grabati
in collo sibi collocare posset.
hic illa, ut decuit cinaediorem,
25 "quaeso," inquit "mihi, mi Catulle, paulum
istos commode: nam volo ad Serapim
deferri." "mane," inquii puellae,
"istud quod modo dixeram me habere,
fugit me ratio: meus sodalis—
30 Cinna est Gaius,—is sibi paravit.
verum, utrum illius an mei, quid ad me?
utor tam bene quam mihi pararim.
sed tu insulsa male et molesta vivis,
per quam non licet esse neglegentem."

Short Answer Questions

Line 1   What is the case and use of *me?* _____

Line 2   What grammatical form is *visum?* _____

Translate *visum.* _____

Line 3   Translate *visum est.* _____

Line 5   What is the uncontracted form of *incidere?*_____

Line 6   What is the mood and tense of *esset,* and in what type of clause is it? _____

Line 8   What is the case and use of *mihi?* _____

Line 10   What is the case and use of *cohorti?* _____

Line 11   What is the case and degree of *unctius?* _____

               What is the mood and tense of *referret?* _____

Line 15   Translate *dicitur.* _____

Line 16   What is the case and use of *puellae?* _____

Line 17   What word does *beatiorem* modify?_____

Line 19   What is the mood and tense of *incidisset?*_____

Line 20   What is the mood and tense of *possem,* and in what type of clause is it? _____

Line 21   What is the case and use of *mi?* _____

Line 25   What case is *mi* and why?_____

Line 27   What is the grammatical use and voice of *deferri?* _____

Line 28   What is the case and use of *me?*_____

Line 31   What is the case and use of *mei?* _____

Line 32   What is the unsyncopated form of *pararim?*_____

Multiple Choice Questions *Suggested time: 20 minutes*

1.   From lines 1–2, it is evident that

       a.   Varus and his girlfriend left the forum

       b.   Varus suggested to his girlfriend that she should leave the forum

       c.   Varus led Catullus out of the forum

       d.   Varus told Catullus that it would be best if he left the forum

2.   In line 2, *otiosum* describes

       a.   Varus

       b.   Catullus

       c.   Varus' girlfriend

       d.   the forum

3.   *scortillum* (line 3) is

       a.   a vocative

       b.   a diminutive

       c.   a syncopated word

       d.   a neuter nominative singular

4. In line 3, *ut* is best translated

   a. as

   c. that

   b. so that

   d. in order to

5. Line 4 contains an example of

   a. asyndeton

   c. an oxymoron

   b. hyperbole

   d. litotes

6. In lines 5–8, the conversations were

   a. between Varus and Catullus alone

   c. started by Varus' girlfriend

   b. about what happened in Bithynia

   d. exceedingly brief

7. In line 9, *ipsis* refers to

   a. Catullus and Varus

   c. Varus and his girlfriend

   b. the litter bearers

   d. the inhabitants of Bithynia

8. *caput unctius* (line 11) refers to

   a. money

   c. brains

   b. dirty hair

   d. oil for cooking

9. In line 16, *ego* refers to

   a. Varus

   c. Catullus

   b. Varus' girlfriend

   d. one of the inhabitants of Bithynia

10. Line 20

    a. is a hypermetric line

    c. has no caesura

    b. contains two elisions

    d. has one synizesis

11. In line 22, there is an example of

    a. synchysis

    c. hendiadys

    b. ellipsis

    d. onomatopoeia

12. From lines 14–23, we learn that

    a. Catullus bought a brand new litter

    c. Catullus wanted to appear well off to Varus' girlfriend

    b. it was not possible for Catullus to lie to Varus' girlfriend

    d. Catullus did not want to buy a litter with a broken leg

13. In line 24, *cinaediorem* refers to

    a. Catullus

    c. Varus' girlfriend

    b. Varus

    d. one of Catullus' friends

14. In lines 24–26, Varus' girlfriend
    a. goes back to Serapis
    c. asks if she can stay at his house
    b. wants to borrow Catullus' litter bearers
    d. speaks to Catullus in an insulting manner

15. In line 28, *istud* refers to
    a. money
    c. litter bearers
    b. reason
    d. Varus

16. From lines 28–32, we learn that
    a. according to Catullus, Cinna bought the litter bearers
    c. it was Cinna who had used Catullus' litter bearers
    b. Catullus did not consider Cinna to be a true friend
    d. recently Cinna had spoken poorly of Catullus

17. In line 33, *tu* refers to
    a. Cinna
    c. Catullus
    b. Varus
    d. Varus' girlfriend

Translation *Suggested time: 4 minutes*

Translate the passage below as literally as possible.

verum, utrum illius an mei, quid ad me?
utor tam bene quam mihi pararim.

_____

_____

_____

_____

Short Essay *Suggested time: 20 minutes*

Indicate how the content and use of language in lines 28–30 demonstrate Catullus' state of mind and feelings at this point in Poem 10.

Support your assertions with references drawn from the poem. All Latin words must be copied or their line numbers provided, AND they must be translated or paraphrased closely enough so that it is clear you understand the Latin. It is your responsibility to convince your reader that you are basing your conclusions on the Latin text and not merely on a general recollection of the passage. Direct your answer to the question; do not merely summarize the passage. Please write your essay on a separate piece of paper.

Long Essay *Suggested time: 30 minutes*

Explain how Catullus' reaction to the situation in which he finds himself changes from the beginning of the poem, through the middle, and then to the end of the poem.

Support your assertions with references drawn from **throughout** the poem. All Latin words must be copied or their line numbers provided, AND they must be translated or paraphrased closely enough so that it is clear you understand the Latin. It is your responsibility to convince your reader that you are basing your conclusions on the Latin text and not merely on a general recollection of the passage. Direct your answer to the question; do not merely summarize the passage. Please write your essay on a separate piece of paper.

Scansion

Scan the following lines and name the meter.

deferri." "mane," inquii puellae,

"istud quod modo dixeram me habere,

CATULLUS 11

Furi et Aureli, comites Catulli,
sive in extremos penetrabit Indos,
litus ut longe resonante Eoa
    tunditur unda,

5   sive in Hyrcanos Arabasve molles,
seu Sagas sagittiferosve Parthos,
sive quae septemgeminus colorat
    aequora Nilus,

sive trans altas gradietur Alpes,
10   Caesaris visens monimenta magni,
Gallicum Rhenum horribile aequor ulti-
    mosque Britannos,

omnia haec, quaecumque feret voluntas
caelitum, temptare simul parati,
15   pauca nuntiate meae puellae
    non bona dicta.

cum suis vivat valeatque moechis,
quos simul complexa tenet trecentos,
nullum amans vere, sed identidem omnium
20   ilia rumpens;

nec meum respectet, ut ante, amorem,
qui illius culpa cecidit velut prati
ultimi flos, praetereunte postquam
    tactus aratro est.

Short Answer Questions

Line 1   What case is *Furi* and *Aureli?* _____

Line 3   What is the grammatical form of *resonante,* and what word does it modify? _____

_____

Line 4   What is the case and use of *unda?* _____

Line 5   What does *-ve* on the end of *Arabas* mean?_____

Line 7   What is the antecedent of *quae?* _____

Line 9   What is the mood and tense of *gradietur*?_____

Line 10   What word does *magni* modify?_____

Line 14   What is the tense, voice, and number of *parati*, and what does it modify? _____

_____

Line 15   What is the mood and number of *nuntiate*? _____

     What is the case and use of *puellae*? _____

Line 17   What is the mood, tense, and use of *vivat*?_____

Line 18   Translate *complexa* literally. _____

Line 22   What is the antecedent of *qui*? _____

     What is the case and use of *culpa*? _____

     To whom does *illius* refer?_____

Multiple Choice Questions *Suggested time: 11 minutes*

1. In line 2, the subject of *penetrabit* is
   a. Catullus
   c. the East
   b. the girl
   d. the wave

2. In line 3, *ut* means
   a. so that
   c. as
   b. that
   d. where

3. According to lines 5–8
   a. the Hyrcanians were considered to be a gentle people
   c. the Parthians were known for fighting with arrows
   b. the Nile watered the Arabians
   d. the Scythians colored their skin

4. In line 13, *omnia haec* refers to
   a. the travels described in previous lines
   c. the will of the heavenly dwellers
   b. the monuments of great Caesar
   d. some unpleasant things that were said

5. Line 16 contains an example of
   a. aposiopesis
   c. hendiadys
   b. litotes
   d. assonance

6. The subject of *valeat* (line 17) refers to

    a. Catullus   b. Caesar

    c. the girl   d. Furius

7. In line 19, *nullum* refers to

    a. *moechis* (line 17)   b. *ilia* (line 20)

    c. *amorem* (line 21)   d. *prati* (line 22)

8. Lines 21–24 contain

    a. two elisions   b. a hiatus

    c. an ecphrasis   d. a simile

9. In lines 23–24, the characters in the poem that are associated with *flos* and *aratro* are

    a. the girl . . . Furius and Aurelius   b. Catullus . . . the girl

    c. Caesar . . . Catullus   d. the Britons . . . the Indians

Translation *Suggested time: 8 minutes*

Translate the passage below as literally as possible.

> **nec meum respectet, ut ante, amorem,**
> **qui illius culpa cecidit velut prati**
> **ultimi flos, praetereunte postquam**
>   **tactus aratro est.**

_____

_____

_____

_____

_____

Short Essay *Suggested time: 20 minutes*

Discuss how the hypermetric lines 11–12 and 22–23 contribute to the meaning of the poem.

Support your assertions with references drawn from **throughout** the poem. All Latin words must be copied or their line numbers provided, AND they must be translated or paraphrased closely enough so that it is clear you understand the Latin. It is your responsibility to convince your reader that you are basing your conclusions on the Latin text and not merely on a general recollection of the passage. Direct your answer to the question; do not merely summarize the passage. Please write your essay on a separate piece of paper.

Long Essay *Suggested time: 30 minutes*

Discuss how the geographical places mentioned in Poem 11 enhance the meaning and tone of Catullus' poem.

Support your assertions with references drawn from **throughout** the poem. All Latin words must be copied or their line numbers provided, AND they must be translated or paraphrased closely enough so that it is clear you understand the Latin. It is your responsibility to convince your reader that you are basing your conclusions on the Latin text and not merely on a general recollection of the passage. Direct your answer to the question; do not merely summarize the passage. Please write your essay on a separate piece of paper.

Scansion

Scan the following lines and name the meter.

omnia haec, quaecumque feret voluntas

caelitum, temptare simul parati,

pauca nuntiate meae puellae

non bona dicta.

CATULLUS 12

Marrucine Asini, manu sinistra
non belle uteris: in ioco atque vino
tollis lintea neglegentiorum.
hoc salsum esse putas? fugit te, inepte:
5   quamvis sordida res et invenusta est.
non credis mihi? crede Pollioni
fratri, qui tua furta vel talento
mutari velit: est enim leporum
differtus puer ac facetiarum.
10   quare aut hendecasyllabos trecentos
exspecta, aut mihi linteum remitte,
quod me non movet aestimatione,
verum est mnemosynum mei sodalis.
nam sudaria Saetaba ex Hiberis
15   miserunt mihi muneri Fabullus
et Veranius: haec amem necesse est
ut Veraniolum meum et Fabullum.

Short Answer Questions

Line 1   What case is *Asini?* _____

               What is the case and use of *manu?* _____

Line 2   What is the person and tense of *uteris?* _____

Line 3   What is the form and case of *neglegentiorum?* _____

Line 4   What is the case and use of *hoc?* _____

               What is the case of *inepte?* _____

Line 6   What is the case and use of *mihi?* _____

Line 7   What is the case and use of *talento?* _____

Line 8   What is the tense, mood, and use of *velit?* _____

Line 11   What is the mood and voice of *remitte?* _____

Line 12   What is the case and use of *aestimatione?* _____

Line 13   What is the case of *mnemosynum?* _____

Line 15   What is the case and use of *muneri?* _____

Line 16   What is the tense, mood, and use of *amem?* _____

Multiple Choice Questions *Suggested time: 10 minutes*

1. From lines 1–3, we learn that Asinius Marrucinus
    a. was being careless during a party
    b. poured the wine with his left hand
    c. was making some naughty jokes
    d. was stealing the napkins of others

2. In lines 4–5, Catullus describes what happened in lines 1–3 as
    a. witty
    b. thoughtful
    c. lacking good taste
    d. dire

3. In line 9, *puer* refers to
    a. Asinius Marrucinus
    b. Pollio
    c. Catullus
    d. a slave at the dinner party

4. *quod* (line 12) refers to
    a. the napkin
    b. a hendecasyllabic poem
    c. what Pollio believes
    d. the foolishness of Marrucinus

5. In line 12, *me* refers to
    a. Pollio
    b. Marrucinus
    c. Catullus
    d. Veranius

6. In line 13, *verum* means
    a. true
    b. but
    c. not only
    d. reminder

7. Line 15 contains an example of
    a. zeugma
    b. hendiadys
    c. alliteration
    d. metonymy

8. All of the following have the same reference **except**
    a. *aestimatione* (line 12)
    b. *mnemosynum* (line 13)
    c. *sudaria* (line 14)
    d. *muneri* (line 15)

Translation *Suggested time: 8 minutes*

Translate the passage below as literally as possible.

> **quamvis sordida res et invenusta est.**
> **non credis mihi? crede Pollioni**
> **fratri, qui tua furta vel talento**
> **mutari velit:**

_____

_____

_____

_____

_____

_____

Long Essay *Suggested time: 30 minutes*

Discuss what personal qualities Poem 12 indicates Catullus prefers to have in his friends and associates.

Support your assertions with references drawn from **throughout** the poem. All Latin words must be copied or their line numbers provided, AND they must be translated or paraphrased closely enough so that it is clear you understand the Latin. It is your responsibility to convince your reader that you are basing your conclusions on the Latin text and not merely on a general recollection of the passage. Direct your answer to the question; do not merely summarize the passage. Please write your essay on a separate piece of paper.

Scansion

Scan the following lines and name the meter.

quare aut hendecasyllabos trecentos

exspecta, aut mihi lineum remitte,

quod me non movet aestimatione,

CATULLUS 13

Cenabis bene, mi Fabulle, apud me
paucis, si tibi di favent, diebus,
si tecum attuleris bonam atque magnam
cenam, non sine candida puella
5   et vino et sale et omnibus cachinnis.
haec si, inquam, attuleris, venuste noster,
cenabis bene; nam tui Catulli
plenus sacculus est aranearum.
sed contra accipies meros amores
10   seu quid suavius elegantiusve est:
nam unguentum dabo, quod meae puellae
donarunt Veneres Cupidinesque,
quod tu cum olfacies, deos rogabis,
totum ut te faciant, Fabulle, nasum.

Short Answer Questions

Line 1   What is the case and use of *mi?* _____

             Translate *apud me.*_____

Line 2   What is the case and use of *diebus?* _____

Line 3   What is the mood and tense of *attuleris?* _____

Line 4   What case is *puella?* _____

Line 6   What is the mood and tense of *inquam?* _____

Line 7   What is the case and use of *Catulli?*_____

Line 9   What is the mood and tense of *accipies?* _____

Line 10   What grammatical form is *suavius?*_____

Line 11   What is the antecedent of *quod?* _____

Line 12   What is the unsycopated form of *donarunt?* _____

Line 13   What part of speech is *cum?* _____

Line 14   What is the mood, tense, and use of *faciant?* _____

Multiple Choice Questions *Suggested time: 10 minutes*

1. The subject of *cenabis* (line 1) refers to

    a. the girl

    c. Fabullus

    b. Catullus

    d. Venus

2. In line 4, there is an example of

    a. litotes

    c. synchysis

    b. alliteration

    d. onomatopoeia

3. Line 5 contains an example of

    a. personification

    c. chiasmus

    b. antithesis

    d. onomatopoeia

4. From lines 1–5, we learn that

    a. Catullus asks Fabullus to bring dinner with him

    c. they will pray to the gods to look favorably on this event

    b. a girl will already be at the dinner when Fabullus arrives

    d. no laughing will be allowed

5. In line 6, *venuste noster* refers to

    a. Fabullus

    c. Catullus

    b. the girl

    d. Venus

6. In lines 7–8, it is revealed that

    a. Catullus is short of funds

    c. Catullus is afraid of spiders

    b. Catullus' house is dirty with cobwebs

    d. Catullus' bag is full of perfume

7. In line 13, *quod* refers to

    a. Fabullus' nose

    c. the perfume

    b. the love that Catullus has for the girl

    d. the gods

8. Line 14 contains an example of

    a. aposiopesis

    c. synchysis

    b. hyperbaton

    d. a simile

Translation *Suggested time: 4 minutes*

Translate the passage below as literally as possible.

> **nam unguentum dabo, quod meae puellae**
> **donarunt Veneres Cupidinesque,**

_____

_____

_____

_____

Short Essay *Suggested time: 20 minutes*

Discuss how the repetition of *cenabis bene* in lines 1 and 7 and the double meaning of *sale* in line 5 enhance the meaning of Poem 13.

Support your assertions with references drawn from the poem. All Latin words must be copied or their line numbers provided, AND they must be translated or paraphrased closely enough so that it is clear you understand the Latin. It is your responsibility to convince your reader that you are basing your conclusions on the Latin text and not merely on a general recollection of the passage. Direct your answer to the question; do not merely summarize the passage. Please write your essay on a separate piece of paper.

Scansion

Scan the following lines and name the meter.

si tecum attuleris bonam atque magnam

cenam, non sine candida puella

et vino et sale et omnibus cachinnis.

CATULLUS 14

Ni te plus oculis meis amarem,
iucundissime Calve, munere isto
odissem te odio Vatiniano:
nam quid feci ego quidve sum locutus,
5   cur me tot male perderes poetis?
isti di mala multa dent clienti,
qui tantum tibi misit impiorum.
quod si, ut suspicor, hoc novum ac repertum
munus dat tibi Sulla litterator,
10   non est mi male, sed bene ac beate,
quod non dispereunt tui labores.
di magni, horribilem et sacrum libellum!
quem tu scilicet ad tuum Catullum
misti continuo, ut die periret,
15   Saturnalibus optimo dierum!
non non hoc tibi, salse, sic abibit.
nam, si luxerit, ad librariorum
curram scrinia, Caesios, Aquinos,
Suffenum, omnia colligam venena,
20   ac te his suppliciis remunerabor.
vos hinc interea valete abite
illuc, unde malum pedem attulistis,
saecli incommoda, pessimi poetae.

Short Answer Questions

Line 1   What is the mood, tense, and use of *amarem*? _____

What is the case and use of *oculis*? _____

Line 2   What is the form and case of *iucundissime*? _____

What is the case and use of *munere*? _____

Line 3   What is the tense, mood, and use of *odissem*? _____

What figure of speech is in this line? _____

Line 5   What is the mood and use of *perderes*? _____

Line 6   What is the mood, tense, and use of *dent*? _____

Line 7   What is the case and use of *impiorum*? _____

Line 8   Translate *quod si.* _____

Line 9   What is the case and use of *tibi?* _____

Line 10   What is the uncontracted form of *mi?* _____

Line 12   What is the case of *di magni?* _____

            What is the case and use of *libellum?* _____

Line 14   What is the unsyncopated form of *misti?* _____

            What is the case and use of *die?* _____

Line 17   What type of condition does *si luxerit* introduce? _____

            What word is the object of *ad?* _____

Line 19   What is the case and use of *venena?* _____

Line 20   Translate *remunerabor.* _____

Line 23   With what word is *incommoda* in apposition?_____

Multiple Choice Questions *Suggested time: 12 minutes*

1. According to lines 1–3,
    a. Calvus received a gift   b. Vatinius accepted a gift
    c. Catullus was given a gift   d. the gift was loved

2. In line 5, *me* refers to
    a. Calvus   b. Vatinius
    c. Catullus   d. Sulla

3. Line 8 contains an example of
    a. hendiadys   b. hypallage
    c. hyperbole   d. hysteron proteron

4. In lines 5–9, Catullus
    a. indicates that scoundrels stole the gift   b. says that bad poets lost the gift
    c. considers who might have given the gift   d. suspects that the client might have taken
                                                       the gift

5. In line 14, *ut* introduces
    a. a result clause   b. a purpose clause
    c. an indirect command   d. a clause of fear

6. From lines 10–15, we learn that
   a. the gift was a book sent on the Saturnalia
   b. the work involved in writing the book was not bad
   c. Catullus thinks he is going to die
   d. the gods sent a horrible thing to Catullus

7. In line 16, *tibi* refers to
   a. Catullus
   b. Suffenus
   c. Calvus
   d. Vatinius

8. In line 19, *venena* refers to
   a. the booksellers
   b. the poetry of bad poets
   c. false statements
   d. book shelves

9. Line 21 contains an example of
   a. aposiopesis
   b. asyndeton
   c. metonymy
   d. anastrophe

10. In lines 21–23, Catullus
    a. asks Calvus and Vatinius to leave with Suffenus, the Caesii, and the Aquini
    b. says goodbye to Calvus and Vatinius
    c. tells the bad poets to go away
    d. indicates that he cannot depart because of his hurt foot

Translation *Suggested time: 10 minutes*

Translate the passage below as literally as possible.

> quod si, ut suspicor, hoc novum ac repertum
> munus dat tibi Sulla litterator,
> non est mi male, sed bene ac beate,
> quod non dispereunt tui labores.
> di magni, horribilem et sacrum libellum!

_____

_____

_____

_____

_____

_____

Long Essay *Suggested time: 30 minutes*

Cui dono lepidum novum libellum
arida modo pumice expolitum?
Corneli, tibi: namque tu solebas
meas esse aliquid putare nugas
5 iam tum, cum ausus es unus Italorum
omne aevum tribus explicare cartis
doctis, Iuppiter, et laboriosis.
quare habe tibi quidquid hoc libelli
qualecumque; quod, <o> patrona virgo,
10 plus uno maneat perenne saeclo.

Catullus 1

Ni te plus oculis meis amarem,
iucundissime Calve, munere isto
odissem te odio Vatiniano:
nam quid feci ego quidve sum locutus,
5 cur me tot male perderes poetis?
isti di mala multa dent clienti,
qui tantum tibi misit impiorum.
quod si, ut suspicor, hoc novum ac repertum
munus dat tibi Sulla litterator,
10 non est mi male, sed bene ac beate,
quod non dispereunt tui labores.
di magni, horribilem et sacrum libellum!
quem tu scilicet ad tuum Catullum
misti continuo, ut die periret,
15 Saturnalibus optimo dierum!
non non hoc tibi, salse, sic abibit.
nam, si luxerit, ad librariorum
curram scrinia, Caesios, Aquinos,
Suffenum, omnia colligam venena,
20 ac te his suppliciis remunerabor.
vos hinc interea valete abite
illuc, unde malum pedem attulistis,
saecli incommoda, pessimi poetae.

Catullus 14

Discuss how in content and language Poem 14 recalls Poem 1.

Support your assertions with references drawn from **throughout** both poems. All Latin words must be copied or their line numbers provided, AND they must be translated or paraphrased closely enough so that it is clear you understand the Latin. It is your responsibility to convince your reader that you are basing your conclusions on the Latin text and not merely on a general recollection of the passage. Direct your answer to the question; do not merely summarize the passage. Please write your essay on a separate piece of paper.

Scansion

Scan the following lines and name the meter.

non est mi male, sed bene ac beate,

quod non dispereunt tui labores.

CATULLUS 22

Suffenus iste, Vare, quem probe nosti,
homo est venustus et dicax et urbanus,
idemque longe plurimos facit versus.
puto esse ego illi milia aut decem aut plura
5   perscripta, nec sic ut fit in palimpseston
relata: cartae regiae, novi libri,
novi umbilici, lora rubra, membranae,
derecta plumbo et pumice omnia aequata.
haec cum legas tu, bellus ille et urbanus
10   Suffenus unus caprimulgus aut fossor
rursus videtur: tantum abhorret ac mutat.
hoc quid putemus esse? qui modo scurra
aut si quid hac re scitius videbatur,
idem infaceto est infacetior rure,
15   simul poemata attigit, neque idem umquam
aeque est beatus ac poema cum scribit:
tam gaudet in se tamque se ipse miratur.
nimirum idem omnes fallimur, neque est quisquam
quem non in aliqua re videre Suffenum
20   possis. suus cuique attributus est error;
sed non videmus manticae quod in tergo est.

Short Answer Questions

Line 1   What is the antecedent of *quem*? _____

What is the unsyncopated form of *nosti*? _____

Line 2   What is the case and use of *dicax*? _____

Line 3   What degree is *plurimos*, and what word does it modify? _____

Line 4   What is the case and use of *illi*? _____

Line 5   Translate *ut*._____

Line 6   What is the case and use of *libri*? _____

Line 8   What is the case and use of *plumbo*? _____

Line 10   What is the case and use of *fossor*? _____

Line 12   What is the mood, tense, and use of *putemus*? _____

Line 13   What is the case and use of *re?*_____

What part of speech and what degree is *scitius?*_____

Line 16   Translate *ac.*_____

Line 20   What is the mood, tense, and use of *possis?*_____

Line 21   What is the case and use of *manticae?*_____

Multiple Choice Questions *Suggested time: 11 minutes*

1. In line 2, *homo* refers to
    a. Varus
    b. an unnamed poet
    c. Catullus
    d. Suffenus

2. From lines 1–3, we learn that Suffenus
    a. talks too much
    b. writes poetry
    c. dislikes Varus
    d. is far away

3. In line 4, *ego* refers to
    a. Catullus
    b. Varus
    c. Suffenus
    d. an unnamed poet who wrote on the palimpsest

4. *palimpseston* (line 5) refers to
    a. the red straps and new decorative end-knobs
    b. the recycled paper on which Suffenus should write
    c. the thin wrapper that was put over the scroll
    d. the ideas that are contained in Suffenus' writings

5. In line 9, *haec* refers to
    a. *milia* (line 4)
    b. *cartae* (line 6)
    c. *lora* (line 7)
    d. *membranae* (line 7)

6. From lines 1–11, we learn that, according to Catullus,
    a. the goat herder Suffenus is quite handsome
    b. a ditch digger could write better than Suffenus
    c. Suffenus' writings are not very well-written
    d. very few poems were written by Suffenus

7. In line 12, *qui* refers to
    a. Catullus
    b. Suffenus
    c. Varus
    d. an unnamed poet

8. It is revealed in line 17 that

    a. Suffenus is a vain person

    b. Suffenus is a good, moral person

    c. Suffenus' poems have a happy tone to them

    d. Suffenus' poems are like those of Catullus

9. In line 21, the *manticae* presumably carries

    a. each man's personal faults

    b. somebody's personal belongings

    c. the scrolls in their wrappers

    d. errors that have been written down

Translation *Suggested time: 5 minutes*

Translate the passage below as literally as possible.

> **qui modo scurra**
> **aut si quid hac re scitius videbatur,**
> **idem infaceto est infacetior rure,**

_____

_____

_____

_____

Long Essay *Suggested time: 30 minutes*

Discuss the various ways Catullus portrays Suffenus' multifaceted personality.

Support your assertions with references drawn from **throughout** the poem. All Latin words must be copied or their line numbers provided, AND they must be translated or paraphrased closely enough so that it is clear you understand the Latin. It is your responsibility to convince your reader that you are basing your conclusions on the Latin text and not merely on a general recollection of the passage. Direct your answer to the question; do not merely summarize the passage. Please write your essay on a separate piece of paper.

Scansion

Scan the following lines and name the meter.

aeque est beatus ac poema cum scribit:

tam gaudet in se tamque se ipse miratur.

nimirum idem omnes fallimur, neque est quisquam

REVIEW ONE

Poems 1, 2, 3, 4, 5, 7, 8, 10, 11, 12, 13, 14, 22

Match these characters that have appeared in Catullus' poems to a fitting description, according to Catullus' view of them.

1. ____ Suffenus

2. ____ Calvus

3. ____ Fabullus

4. ____ Asinius Marrucinus

5. ____ Gaius Cinna

6. ____ Asinius Pollio

7. ____ Furius

8. ____ Cornelius

9. ____ Varus

10. ____ Veranius

A. is est leporum differtus

B. comes Catulli

C. amicus qui Catullum e foro duxit

D. auctor qui poemis Catulli fruitur

E. venustus sed non bene scribit

F. sodalis qui munus Catullo ex Hispania misit

G. is in Vatinium orationem habuit

H. sodalis qui in Bithynia cum Catullo fuerat

I. eum ad cenam Catullus invitavit

J. vir ineptus qui lintea tollit

Below are quotations from Catullus' poems. Explain to what the words in bold refer.

1. meas esse aliquid putare **nugas**_____

2. **munus** dat tibi Sulla litterator, _____

3. nam unguentum dabo, quod **meae puellae**_____

4. conturbabimus **illa**, ne sciamus, _____

5. quicum ludere, **quem** in sinu tenere, _____

6. tuo imbuisse **palmulas** in aequore,_____

7. qui illius **culpa** cecidit velut prati _____

8. tam gaudet in **se** tamque **se ipse** miratur. _____

9. verum est **mnemosynum** mei sodalis. _____

10. non possem **octo homines** parare **rectos**. _____

11. **quae** nec pernumerare curiosi _____

12. **nox** est perpetua una dormienda. _____

13. at **tu** dolebis, cum rogaberis nulla. _____

14. nec **sese** a gremio illius movebat, _____

Catullus often uses vocatives in his poetry. Transform each person's name from the first matching exercise on page 58 into the vocative case.

1. Suffenus _____

2. Calvus _____

3. Fabullus _____

4. Asinius Marrucinus _____

5. Gaius Cinna _____

6. Asinius Pollio _____

7. Furius _____

8. Cornelius _____

9. Varus _____

10. Veranius _____

Long Essay *Suggested time: 30 minutes*

Marrucine Asini, manu sinistra
non belle uteris: in ioco atque vino
tollis lintea neglegentiorum.
hoc salsum esse putas? fugit te, inepte:
5   quamvis sordida res et invenusta est.
non credis mihi? crede Pollioni
fratri, qui tua furta vel talento
mutari velit: est enim leporum
differtus puer ac facetiarum.
10   quare aut hendecasyllabos trecentos
exspecta, aut mihi linteum remitte,
quod me non movet aestimatione,
verum est mnemosynum mei sodalis.
nam sudaria Saetaba ex Hiberis
15   miserunt mihi muneri Fabullus
et Veranius: haec amem necesse est
ut Veraniolum meum et Fabullum.

Catullus 12

Cenabis bene, mi Fabulle, apud me
paucis, si tibi di favent, diebus,
si tecum attuleris bonam atque magnam
cenam, non sine candida puella
5   et vino et sale et omnibus cachinnis.
haec si, inquam, attuleris, venuste noster,
cenabis bene; nam tui Catulli
plenus sacculus est aranearum.
sed contra accipies meros amores
10   seu quid suavius elegantiusve est:
nam unguentum dabo, quod meae puellae
donarunt Veneres Cupidinesque,
quod tu cum olfacies, deos rogabis,
totum ut te faciant, Fabulle, nasum.

Catullus 13

Ni te plus oculis meis amarem,
iucundissime Calve, munere isto
odissem te odio Vatiniano:
nam quid feci ego quidve sum locutus,
5   cur me tot male perderes poetis?
isti di mala multa dent clienti,
qui tantum tibi misit impiorum.
quod si, ut suspicor, hoc novum ac repertum
munus dat tibi Sulla litterator,
10   non est mi male, sed bene ac beate,
quod non dispereunt tui labores.
di magni, horribilem et sacrum libellum!
quem tu scilicet ad tuum Catullum
misti continuo, ut die periret,
15   Saturnalibus optimo dierum!
non non hoc tibi, salse, sic abibit.
nam, si luxerit, ad librariorum
curram scrinia, Caesios, Aquinos,
Suffenum, omnia colligam venena,
20   ac te his suppliciis remunerabor.
vos hinc interea valete abite
illuc, unde malum pedem attulistis,
saecli incommoda, pessimi poetae.

Catullus 14

Catullus has organized his poetry so that a series of poems often sustains a predominant theme or themes. Discuss the themes that interconnect Poems 12, 13, and 14.

Support your assertions with references drawn from **throughout** the poems. All Latin words must be copied or their line numbers provided, AND they must be translated or paraphrased closely enough so that it is clear you understand the Latin. It is your responsibility to convince your reader that you are basing your conclusions on the Latin text and not merely on a general recollection of the passage. Direct your answer to the question; do not merely summarize the passage. Please write your essay on a separate piece of paper.

Scansion

Scan each of the following sets of lines and name the meter for each.

A.

> di magni, horribilem et sacrum libellum!
>
> quem tu scilicet ad tuum Catullum
>
> misti continuo, ut die periret,
>
> Saturnalibus optimo dierum!

B.

> sive in Hyrcanos Arabasve molles,
>
> seu Sagas sagittiferosve Parthos,
>
> sive quae septemgeminus colorat
>
> > aequora Nilus,

CATULLUS 30

Alfene immemor atque unanimis false sodalibus,
iam te nil miseret, dure, tui dulcis amiculi?
iam me prodere, iam non dubitas fallere, perfide?
nec facta impia fallacum hominum caelicolis placent.
5   quae tu neglegis ac me miserum deseris in malis.
eheu quid faciant, dic, homines cuive habeant fidem?
certe tute iubebas animam tradere, inique, <me>
inducens in amorem, quasi tuta omnia mi forent.
idem nunc retrahis te ac tua dicta omnia factaque
10   ventos irrita ferre ac nebulas aereas sinis.
si tu oblitus es, at di meminerunt, meminit Fides,
quae te ut paeniteat postmodo facti faciet tui.

Short Answer Questions

Line 1   What is the case and use of *sodalibus?* _____

What is the case and use of *Alfene?* _____

Line 2   What is the case and use of *amiculi?* _____

Translate *amiculi.* _____

Line 3   What is the mood, voice, and use of *prodere?* _____

Line 4   What is the case and use of *facta?* _____

Line 6   What is the mood and use of *faciant?* _____

Line 7   Translate *tute.* _____

Line 8   For what words is *forent* the alternative form? _____

For what word is *mi* the alternative form? _____

Line 10   What word does *irrita* modify? _____

Line 11   From what Latin word does *oblitus* come? _____

Line 12   What is the mood, tense, and use of *paeniteat?* _____

Multiple Choice Questions *Suggested time: 6 minutes*

1. In line 2, *te* refers to

    a. Alfenus

    b. the friend

    c. Catullus

    d. a god

2. In lines 2–3, there is an example of

    a. chiasmus

    b. aposiopesis

    c. anaphora

    d. alliteration

3. From lines 1–4, we learn that

    a. Alfenus and his friends are forgetful

    b. Alfenus has been a disloyal friend

    c. Alfenus cannot please the gods

    d. Alfenus feels pity for his friends

4. In lines 7–10, Catullus states that

    a. the gods encouraged him to fall in love

    b. he felt the time was safe for him to fall in love

    c. falling in love was like riding winds and clouds

    d. there was encouragement for him to fall in love

5. In line 12, there is an example of

    a. asyndeton

    b. a simile

    c. hendiadys

    d. alliteration

Translation *Suggested time: 5 minutes*

Translate the passage below as literally as possible.

> **quae tu neglegis ac me miserum deseris in malis.**
> **eheu quid faciant, dic, homines cuive habeant fidem?**

_____

_____

_____

_____

Short Essay *Suggested time: 20 minutes*

In Poem 30 Catullus makes use of several words and phrases to great effect. Describe the significance of one of the following sets of words/phrases for the poem as a whole.

Lines 1–3—false . . . dure . . . perfide
Line 5—me miserum
Line 11—oblitus es, at di meminerunt

Support your assertions with references drawn from the poem. All Latin words must be copied or their line numbers provided, AND they must be translated or paraphrased closely enough so that it is clear you understand the Latin. It is your responsibility to convince your reader that you are basing your conclusions on the Latin text and not merely on a general recollection of the passage. Direct your answer to the question; do not merely summarize the passage. Please write your essay on a separate piece of paper.

Scansion

Scan the following lines and name the non-AP meter.

iam me prodere, iam non dubitas fallere, perfide?

nec facta impia fallacum hominum caelicolis placent.

quae tu neglegis ac me miserum deseris in malis.

CATULLUS 31

      Paene insularum, Sirmio, insularumque
      ocelle, quascumque in liquentibus stagnis
      marique vasto fert uterque Neptunus,
      quam te libenter quamque laetus inviso
5   vix mi ipse credens Thuniam atque Bithunos
      liquisse campos et videre te in tuto.
      o quid solutis est beatius curis,
      cum mens onus reponit, ac peregrino
      labore fessi venimus larem ad nostrum,
10   desideratoque acquiescimus lecto?
      hoc est quod unum est pro laboribus tantis.
      salve, o venusta Sirmio, atque ero gaude
      gaudente, vosque, o Lydiae lacus undae,
      ridete quidquid est domi cachinnorum.

Short Answer Questions

Line 1   What is the case and use of *Sirmio?* _____

Line 2   From what Latin word is the diminutive *ocelle* formed? _____

                What is the case and translation of *ocelle?* _____

                Of what verb is *quascumque* the object? _____

Line 3   What is the case and use of *mari?* _____

Line 4   Translate *quam.* _____

                What part of speech is *libenter?* _____

Line 5   What is the case, use, and translation of *mi?* _____

                What does *ipse* modify, and how is this adjective translated? _____

Line 6   What is the tense and voice of *liquisse?* _____

                Translate *liquisse.* _____

Line 7   What case and form is *beatius?* _____

                What is the case and use of *curis?* _____

Line 8   What is the case and use of *onus?* _____

Line 9   What does *fessi* modify? _____

Line 10   What is the case and use of *lecto?* _____

Line 11   What is the antecedent of *quod?* _____

Line 12   What is the case and use of *ero?* _____

Line 13   What is the case and form of *gaudente,* and what does it modify? _____

Line 14   What is the case and use of *domi?* _____

           What is the case and use of *cachinnorum?* _____

Multiple Choice Questions *Suggested time: 10 minutes*

1. In line 2, *quascumque* refers to
   a. islands and peninsulas
   b. liquid standing water
   c. the sea
   d. Neptune's eye

2. In line 4, *te* refers to
   a. Catullus
   b. Neptune
   c. Sirmio
   d. Thynia

3. From lines 1–6, we learn that
   a. Neptune has been keeping the waters calm
   b. the eye of the storm is near the islands
   c. Sirmio is glad to see that Catullus is safe
   d. Catullus has returned from Thynia and Bithynia

4. In line 7, there is an example of
   a. synchysis
   b. litotes
   c. onomatopeia
   d. ellipsis

5. Line 9 contains an example of
   a. aposiopesis
   b. metonymy
   c. a simile
   d. anaphora

6. From lines 7–10, it is clear that Catullus
   a. dislikes working in foreign countries
   b. wants to work on repairing his house
   c. is glad to be able to sleep in his own bed at home
   d. feels the solution is a cause for great concern

CATULLUS

7. In line 13, *vos* refers to

    a. water
    c. rejoicing

    b. Sirmio
    d. Lydia

8. In lines 11–14, Catullus says that he feels

    a. regretful
    c. concerned

    b. happy
    d. ambivalent

Translation *Suggested time: 6 minutes*

Translate the passage below as literally as possible.

> **quam te libenter quamque laetus inviso**
> **vix mi ipse credens Thuniam atque Bithunos**
> **liquisse campos et videre te in tuto.**

_____

_____

_____

_____

_____

_____

Long Essay *Suggested time: 30 minutes*

Many words in Poem 31 contain the letter "l." Discuss the interplay between the repetition of this sound and the water imagery that pervades the poem.

Support your assertions with references drawn from **throughout** the poem. All Latin words must be copied or their line numbers provided, AND they must be translated or paraphrased closely enough so that it is clear you understand the Latin. It is your responsibility to convince your reader that you are basing your conclusions on the Latin text and not merely on a general recollection of the passage. Direct your answer to the question; do not merely summarize the passage. Please write your essay on a separate piece of paper.

Scansion

Scan the following lines and identify the non-AP meter.

cum mens onus reponit, ac peregrino

labore fessi venimus larem ad nostrum,

desideratoque acquiescimus lecto?

CATULLUS 35

Poetae tenero, meo sodali,
velim Caecilio, papyre, dicas
Veronam veniat, Novi relinquens
Comi moenia Lariumque litus.
5   nam quasdam volo cogitationes
amici accipiat sui meique.
quare, si sapiet, viam vorabit,
quamvis candida milies puella
euntem revocet, manusque collo
10   ambas iniciens roget morari.
quae nunc, si mihi vera nuntiantur,
illum deperit impotente amore.
nam quo tempore legit incohatam
Dindymi dominam, ex eo misellae
15   ignes interiorem edunt medullam.
ignosco tibi, Sapphica puella
musa doctior: est enim venuste
Magna Caecilio incohata Mater.

Short Answer Questions

Line 1   What is the case and use of *poetae*? _____

Line 2   What is the mood, tense, and use of *velim*? _____

                What is the mood and use of *dicas*? _____

Line 3   What is the case and use of *Veronam*? _____

                What is the mood and use of *veniat*? _____

Line 4   What is the case and use of *litus*? _____

Line 5   Of what verb is *cogitationes* the object? _____

Line 7   What type of conditional sentence is in this line?_____

Line 9   What is the case and use of *collo*? _____

Line 10   What word does *ambas* modify?_____

Line 11   Translate *vera*. _____

Line 12   What is the case and use of *amore*? _____

Line 13   What is the mood, tense, and voice of *incohatam*? _____

Line 14   Of what verb is *dominam* the object? _____

Line 15   What figure of speech is in this line? _____

Line 16   What is the case and use of *tibi*? _____

                   What is the case and use of *Sapphica puella?*_____

Line 17   Translate *venuste.* _____

Line 18   What is the case and use of *Caecilio?* _____

Multiple Choice Questions *Suggested time: 13 minutes*

1. In lines 1–2, Catullus is speaking about

   a. one person

   b. two different persons

   c. three different persons

   d. four different persons

2. In lines 2–4, there is an example of

   a. apostrophe

   b. chiasmus

   c. polysyndeton

   d. an oxymoron

3. Line 6 contains an example of

   a. synchysis

   b. assonance

   c. enjambment

   d. zeugma

4. According to lines 1–6,

   a. Caecilius says that Catullus is a tender poet and his friend

   b. Catullus wants to share some thoughts with Caecilius in Verona

   c. Catullus likes Caecilius' poem about the walls of New Como

   d. Caecilius has a piece of papyrus he wants to show Catullus

5. In line 8, *puella r*efers to

   a. Lesbia

   b. the Great Mother

   c. Sappho

   d. Caecilius' girlfriend

6. From lines 7–10, we discover that

   a. he would be wise to embrace her

   b. he delays his departure

   c. she does not want him to leave

   d. she refuses to hug him

7. In line 11, *quae* refers to

   a. the truth

   b. the girl

   c. her hands

   d. his love

8. In line 14, *Dindymi dominam* refers to

    a. the lady of the house   b. a mountain in Rome

    c. a piece of writing   d. Sappho

9. *miselle* (line 14) is an example of a

    a. diminutive   b. locative

    c. hyperbaton   d. metaphor

10. In line 16, *tibi* refers to

    a. Caecilius   b. the girl

    c. Sappho   d. the muse

11. By the end of the poem, it is clear that

    a. Caecilius' poem is not complete   b. Catullus is suffering from the fires of love

    c. the girl wants forgiveness   d. Caecilius and Catullus have decided to go on a long journey to worship the Magna Mater

Translation *Suggested time: 6 minutes*

Translate the passage below as literally as possible.

> **nam quo tempore legit incohatam**
> **Dindymi dominam, ex eo misellae**
> **ignes interiorem edunt medullam.**

_____

_____

_____

_____

_____

Short Essay *Suggested time: 20 minutes*

Catullus uses many figures of speech to enhance the meaning of Poem 35. Cite and translate at least two figures of speech and explain the effect each has on the poem.

Support your assertions with references drawn from the poem. All Latin words must be copied or their line numbers provided, AND they must be translated or paraphrased closely enough so that it is clear you understand the Latin. It is your responsibility to convince your reader that you are basing your conclusions on the Latin text and not merely on a general recollection of the passage. Direct your answer to the question; do not merely summarize the passage. Please write your essay on a separate piece of paper.

Scansion

Scan the following lines and name the meter.

amici accipiat sui meique.

quare, si sapiet, viam vorabit,

quamvis candida milies puella

CATULLUS 36

Annales Volusi, cacata carta,
votum solvite pro mea puella.
nam sanctae Veneri Cupidinique
vovit, si sibi restitutus essem
5   desissemque truces vibrare iambos,
electissima pessimi poetae
scripta tardipedi deo daturam
infelicibus ustulanda lignis.
et hoc pessima se puella vidit
10   iocose lepide vovere divis.
nunc o caeruleo creata ponto,
quae sanctum Idalium Uriosque apertos
quaeque Ancona Cnidumque harundinosam
colis quaeque Amathunta quaeque Golgos
15   quaeque Durrachium Hadriae tabernam,
acceptum face redditumque votum,
si non illepidum neque invenustum est.
at vos interea venite in ignem,
pleni ruris et inficetiarum
20   annales Volusi, cacata carta.

Short Answer Questions

Line 1   What is the case and use of *Annales?* _____

              What is in apposition with *Annales?* _____

Line 2   What is the tense, voice, and number of *solvite?* _____

Line 3   What is the case and use of *Veneri?* _____

Line 4   What is the mood, tense, voice, and number of *restitutus essem?* _____

_____

Line 5   What does *truces* modify? _____

Line 6   What does *electissima* modify? _____

Line 7   What is the case and use of *deo?* _____

Line 8   What tense and form is *ustulanda?* _____

Line 9   What is the case and use of *se?* _____

Line 10   What part of speech is *lepide*? _____

Line 11   What is the case and use of *ponto*? _____

Line 13   What is the case and use of *Ancona*? _____

Line 16   What form is *face*? _____

                What word does *acceptum* modify? _____

Line 19   What word does *pleni* modify? _____

Multiple Choice Questions *Suggested time: 12 minutes*

1. What are *Annales* (line 1)?
   a. pornographic writings
   c. yearly records of events
   b. Volusius's letters to his girlfriend
   d. sacred vows written on paper

2. In line 2, *puella* refers to
   a. Lesbia
   c. Amathunta
   b. Venus
   d. the unnamed girlfriend of Volusius

3. *sibi* (line 4) refers to
   a. Volusius
   c. Cupid
   b. Catullus
   d. Lesbia

4. In line 7, *daturam* refers to
   a. *carta* (line 1)
   c. *poetae* (line 6)
   b. *mea puella* (line 2)
   d. *scripta* (line 7)

5. From lines 3–8, it becomes clear that
   a. Catullus is going to write some fierce poems
   c. a bad poet will give some writings to a god
   b. Venus and Cupid intend to reunite the lovers
   d. a vow had been made to burn some writings

6. Line 10 contains an example of
   a. asyndeton
   c. metonymy
   b. metaphor
   d. hyperbaton

7. In line 11, to whom does *creata* refer?
   a. the girl
   c. Ancona
   b. Venus
   d. Idalium

8. In lines 12–15, there is an example of

    a. a simile

    b. alliteration

    c. hysteron proteron

    d. anaphora

9. Line 17 contains an example of

    a. litotes

    b. hendiadys

    c. hypallage

    d. a golden line

10. In line 18, *vos* refers to

    a. Catullus and Lesbia

    b. all the places mentioned in the preceeding lines

    c. Volusius' writings

    d. Venus and Cupid

Translation *Suggested time: 6 minutes*

Translate the passage below as literally as possible.

> **at vos interea venite in ignem,**
> **pleni ruris et inficetiarum**
> **annales Volusi, cacata carta.**

_____

_____

_____

_____

_____

_____

Long Essay *Suggested time: 30 minutes*

Discuss the ways in which Catullus integrates the elements of love, poetry, and humor in Poem 36.

Support your assertions with references drawn from **throughout** the poem. All Latin words must be copied or their line numbers provided, AND they must be translated or paraphrased closely enough so that it is clear you understand the Latin. It is your responsibility to convince your reader that you are basing your conclusions on the Latin text and not merely on a general recollection of the passage. Direct your answer to the question; do not merely summarize the passage. Please write your essay on a separate piece of paper.

Scansion

Scan the following lines and name the meter.

iocose lepide vovere divis.

nunc o caeruleo creata ponto,

quae sanctum Idalium Uriosque apertos

CATULLUS 40

Quaenam te mala mens, miselle Ravide,
agit praecipitem in meos iambos?
quis deus tibi non bene advocatus
vecordem parat excitare rixam?
5   an ut pervenias in ora vulgi?
quid vis? qualubet esse notus optas?
eris, quandoquidem meos amores
cum longa voluisti amare poena.

Short Answer Questions

Line 1   What is the case and use of *Ravide?* _____

Line 2   What word does *praecipitem* modify? _____

Line 3   What is the case and use of *tibi?* _____

Line 4   What does *vecordem* modify? _____

Line 5   What is the mood, tense, and voice of *pervenias?* _____

Line 6   Translate *vis.* _____

Line 8   What is the direct object of *amare?* _____

Multiple Choice Questions *Suggested time: 6 minutes*

1. Line 1 contains an example of
    a. chiasmus
    c. anastrophe
    b. alliteration
    d. polyptoton

2. In line 2, to what does *iambos* refer?
    a. poor Ravidus
    c. your evil mind
    b. a swift movement forward
    d. lines of verse

3. From lines 1–4, we learn that
    a. Catullus is angry with Ravidus
    c. Catullus has been writing some poems too quickly
    b. a god will bring an end to this matter
    d. Ravidus considers Catullus to be an advocate

4. In lines 5–6, there is an example of

    a. hendiadys

    c. asyndeton

    b. rhetorical questions

    d. a simile

5. In line 7, *meos amores* refers to

    a. Catullus' love of poetry

    c. Ravidus' love of fame

    b. Catullus' lover

    d. Cupid

Translation *Suggested time: 5 minutes*

Translate the passage below as literally as possible.

> **an ut pervenias in ora vulgi?**
> **quid vis? qualubet esse notus optas?**

_____

_____

_____

Short Essay *Suggested time: 20 minutes*

Discuss the ways in which Catullus characterizes Ravidus.

Support your assertions with references drawn from **throughout** the poem. All Latin words must be copied or their line numbers provided, AND they must be translated or paraphrased closely enough so that it is clear you understand the Latin. It is your responsibility to convince your reader that you are basing your conclusions on the Latin text and not merely on a general recollection of the passage. Direct your answer to the question; do not merely summarize the passage. Please write your essay on a separate piece of paper.

Scansion

Scan the following lines and name the meter.

> **agit praecipitem in meos iambos?**

> **quis deus tibi non bene advocatus**

> **vecordem parat excitare rixam?**

CATULLUS 43

Salve, nec minimo puella naso
nec bello pede nec nigris ocellis
nec longis digitis nec ore sicco
nec sane nimis elegante lingua,
5   decoctoris amica Formiani.
ten provincia narrat esse bellam?
tecum Lesbia nostra comparatur?
o saeclum insapiens et infacetum!

Short Answer Questions

Line 1   What is the case and use of *naso?* _____

Line 2   Translate *ocellis.*_____

Line 3   What word does *sicco* modify?_____

Line 4   What part of speech is *nimis?* _____

Line 5   What word does *Formiani* modify? _____

           What is the case and use of *amica?* _____

Line 6   What word does *bellam* modify? _____

Line 8   What is the case and use of *saeclum?* _____

Multiple Choice Questions *Suggested time: 6 minutes*

1.   What figure of speech is reiterated several times in lines 1–4?
     a. synchysis   b. litotes
     c. metaphor   d. onomatopeia

2.   From lines 1–5, we learn that the girl
     a. has a very small nose and black eyes   b. does not know the man from Formiae
     c. speaks in a quite inelegant fashion   d. likes her short fingers and wet mouth

3.   Line 6 contains an example of
     a. personification   b. metaphor
     c. ellipsis   d. tricolon crescens

4. In line 6, *ten* is

    a. the shortened form of *tene (te + ne)*   b. the imperative singular of *teneo*

    c. an adverb   d. a Greek accusative

5. By the end of Poem 43, it is evident that Catullus thinks

    a. people from the provinces are beautiful   b. the girlfriend of the man from Formiae is beautiful

    c. other girls cannot compare in beauty to Lesbia   d. his generation wants to go to war

Translation *Suggested time: 6 minutes*

Translate the passage below as literally as possible.

> ten provincia narrat esse bellam?
> tecum Lesbia nostra comparatur?
> o saeclum insapiens et infacetum!

_____

_____

_____

_____

_____

Short Essay *Suggested time: 20 minutes*

Discuss the qualities Catullus considers essential for a beautiful woman and how this poem defines them.

Support your assertions with references drawn from **throughout** the poem. All Latin words must be copied or their line numbers provided, AND they must be translated or paraphrased closely enough so that it is clear you understand the Latin. It is your responsibility to convince your reader that you are basing your conclusions on the Latin text and not merely on a general recollection of the passage. Direct your answer to the question; do not merely summarize the passage. Please write your essay on a separate piece of paper.

Scansion

Scan the following lines and name the meter.

nec sane nimis elegante lingua,

decoctoris amica Formiani.

CATULLUS 44

O funde noster seu Sabine seu Tiburs
(nam te esse Tiburtem autumant, quibus non est
cordi Catullum laedere; at quibus cordi est,
quovis Sabinum pignore esse contendunt),
5   sed seu Sabine sive verius Tiburs,
fui libenter in tua suburbana
villa, malamque pectore expuli tussim,
non inmerenti quam mihi meus venter,
dum sumptuosas appeto, dedit, cenas.
10 nam, Sestianus dum volo esse conviva,
orationem in Antium petitorem
plenam veneni et pestilentiae legi.
hic me gravedo frigida et frequens tussis
quassavit usque, dum in tuum sinum fugi,
15 et me recuravi otioque et urtica.
quare refectus maximas tibi grates
ago, meum quod non es ulta peccatum.
nec deprecor iam, si nefaria scripta
Sesti recepso, quin gravedinem et tussim
20 non mi, sed ipsi Sestio ferat frigus,
qui tunc vocat me, cum malum librum legi.

Short Answer Questions

Line 1   What is the case and use of *funde?* _____

Line 2   What is the case and use of *te?* _____

           What is the case and use of *quibus?* _____

Line 3   What is the case and use of *cordi?* _____

           Translate *at.* _____

Line 4   What is the case and use of *pignore?* _____

Line 6   What is the tense and person of *fui?* _____

Line 7   What is the case and use of *pectore?* _____

Line 8   What is the antecedent of *quam?* _____

           What word does *inmerenti* modify? _____

Line 9   What is the subject of *dedit?* _____

Line 10   What word does *Sestianus* modify? _____

Line 11   Translate *in.* _____

Line 12   What does *plenam* modify? _____

Line 13   What is the case and use of *gravedo?* _____

Line 15   Translate *me.* _____

                 What is the case and use of *urtica?* _____

Line 16   What is the grammatical form of *refectus?* _____

Line 17   Translate *es ulta.* _____

Line 19   Translate *quin.* _____

Line 20   What is the case and use of *mi?* _____

Line 21   Translate *cum.* _____

Multiple Choice Questions *Suggested time: 12 minutes*

1.   In line 2, *te* refers to
     a. Catullus   b. Sestius
     c. Catullus' estate   d. the pledge

2.   From lines 1–5, we learn that
     a. Catullus' estate is quite ordinary   b. Catullus has a country estate
     c. Catullus has been hurt at his estate   d. Catullus is at his estate because he is
                                                      sick at heart

3.   In lines 6–12, it is explained that Catullus
     a. experienced food poisoning from a   b. suffered from an upset stomach from too
        fancy dinner   much food
     c. caught a cold and a cough from reading   d. became sick because of the foul oration
        an oration   of Antius

4.   Line 13 contains an example of
     a. chiasmus   b. personification
     c. hendiadys   d. hysteron proteron

5.   In line 14, *tuum sinum* refers to
     a. Catullus' friend Sestius   b. Catullus' writings
     c. Catullus' estate   d. Catullus' friend Antius

6. In line 15, there is an example of
   a. zeugma
   b. asyndeton
   c. hyperbole
   d. polyptoton

7. From lines 15–17, we learn that Catullus
   a. recovered from being sick
   b. thanked Sestius for visiting him
   c. did not blame Antius for his illness
   d. felt that he had been punished

8. In line 18, *nefaria scripta* refer to
   a. Antius' prose
   b. Catullus' poems
   c. Sestius' writings
   d. Catullus' books

9. Line 20 contains an example of
   a. anastrophe
   b. alliteration
   c. litotes
   d. synecdoche

10. In this poem Catullus equates
    a. bad writing with catching cold
    b. his estate with a place to hold dinner parties
    c. Sabine with an affluent neighborhood
    d. leisure with dining with Sestius

Translation *Suggested time: 8 minutes*

Translate the passage below as literally as possible.

> **fui libenter in tua suburbana**
> **villa, malamque pectore expuli tussim,**
> **non inmerenti quam mihi meus venter,**
> **dum sumptuosas appeto, dedit, cenas.**

_____

_____

_____

_____

_____

_____

Short Essay *Suggested time: 20 minutes*

Discuss how the repetition of the words *tussis* and *tussim* enhance the poem.

Support your assertions with references drawn from **throughout** the poem. All Latin words must be copied or their line numbers provided, AND they must be translated or paraphrased closely enough so that it is clear you understand the Latin. It is your responsibility to convince your reader that you are basing your conclusions on the Latin text and not merely on a general recollection of the passage. Direct your answer to the question; do not merely summarize the passage. Please write your essay on a separate piece of paper.

Scansion

Scan the following lines and identify the non-AP meter.

hic me gravedo frigida et frequens tussis

quassavit usque, dum in tuum sinum fugi,

et me recuravi otioque et urtica.

CATULLUS 45

Acmen Septimius suos amores
tenens in gremio "mea" inquit "Acme,
ni te perdite amo atque amare porro
omnes sum assidue paratus annos,
5   quantum qui pote plurimum perire,
solus in Libya Indiaque tosta
caesio veniam obvius leoni."
hoc ut dixit, Amor sinistra ut ante
dextra sternuit approbationem.
10   at Acme leviter caput reflectens
et dulcis pueri ebrios ocellos
illo purpureo ore suaviata,
"sic," inquit "mea vita Septimille,
huic uni domino usque serviamus,
15   ut multo mihi maior acriorque
ignis mollibus ardet in medullis."
hoc ut dixit, Amor sinistra ut ante
dextra sternuit approbationem.
nunc ab auspicio bono profecti
20   mutuis animis amant amantur.
unam Septimius misellus Acmen
mavult quam Syrias Britanniasque:
uno in Septimio fidelis Acme
facit delicias libidinesque.
25   quis ullos homines beatiores
vidit, quis Venerem auspicatiorem?

Short Answer Questions

Line 1   What is the case and use of *Acmen?* _____

Line 2   What word does *tenens* modify? _____

Line 3   To what verb is *amare* complementary?_____

Line 4   What is the case and use of *annos?* _____

Line 7   What is the mood and tense of *veniam?* _____

           What is the case and use of *leoni?* _____

Line 8   Translate *ut* as it is used each time in this line. _____

Line 9   What is the subject of *sternuit?* _____

Line 10   What is the case and use of *caput?* _____

Line 11   Translate *ocellos.* _____

Line 12   What is the case and use of *ore?* _____

            Translate *suaviata.* _____

Line 14   What is the case of *uni,* and what word does it modify? _____

            What is the mood, tense, and use of *serviamus?* _____

Line 15   What is the case and use of *multo?* _____

            What is the case and degree of *maior?* _____

Line 16   What word does *mollibus* modify? _____

Line 19   Translate *profecti.* _____

Line 21   What does *unam* modify? _____

Line 23   What does *fidelis* modify? _____

Line 25   What is the case and degree of *beatiores?* _____

Multiple Choice Questions *Suggested time: 11 minutes*

1. In line 3, *te* refers to
    a. Catullus   b. Acme
    c. Septimius   d. the lion

2. Line 3 contains an example of
    a. polysyndeton   b. zeugma
    c. apostrophe   d. polyptoton

3. In line 5, there is an example of
    a. asyndeton   b. hendiadys
    c. onomatopeia   d. alliteration

4. From lines 1–7, we learn that
    a. Septimius has seen a gray-eyed lion   b. Acme is sitting on Septimius' lap
    c. Acme and Septimius are expressing   d. Septimius must travel to Libya and India
       their love for one another

5. From lines 10–16, we learn that

    a. Septimius is Acme's master

    b. Acme keeps turning her head from side to side

    c. Septimius is afraid that he will lose his life in a fire in the house

    d. Acme is kissing Septimius

6. In line 16, there is an example of

    a. a metaphor

    b. chiasmus

    c. asyndeton

    d. an oxymoron

7. Which of these figures of speech is **not** present in line 20?

    a. polyptoton

    b. assonance

    c. chiasmus

    d. asyndeton

8. From lines 17–24, it is evident that

    a. Acme and Septimius are in love

    b. Cupid does not approve

    c. Septimius must go to Syria and Britain

    d. Acme is not being faithful to Septimius

9. Which of these figures of speech is **not** present in lines 25–26?

    a. anaphora

    b. rhetorical question

    c. hyperbole

    d. synecdoche

Translation *Suggested time: 8 minutes*

Translate the passage below as literally as possible.

> **unam Septimius misellus Acmen**
> **mavult quam Syrias Britanniasque:**
> **uno in Septimio fidelis Acme**
> **facit delicias libidinesque.**

_____

_____

_____

_____

_____

_____

Short Essay *Suggested time: 20 minutes*

Explain how Catullus' use of sound in line 3 and again in line 5 augments the meaning of the surrounding lines.

Support your assertions with references drawn from the poem. All Latin words must be copied or their line numbers provided, AND they must be translated or paraphrased closely enough so that it is clear you understand the Latin. It is your responsibility to convince your reader that you are basing your conclusions on the Latin text and not merely on a general recollection of the passage. Direct your answer to the question; do not merely summarize the passage. Please write your essay on a separate piece of paper.

Long Essay *Suggested time: 30 minutes*

Poem 45 exhibits a clearly defined structural organization. Identify the organization and discuss how the different parts correspond and respond thematically to one another.

Support your assertions with references drawn from **throughout** the poem. All Latin words must be copied or their line numbers provided, AND they must be translated or paraphrased closely enough so that it is clear you understand the Latin. It is your responsibility to convince your reader that you are basing your conclusions on the Latin text and not merely on a general recollection of the passage. Direct your answer to the question; do not merely summarize the passage. Please write your essay on a separate piece of paper.

Scansion

Scan the following lines and name the meter.

huic uni domino usque serviamus,

ut multo mihi maior acriorque

ignis mollibus ardet in medullis.

CATULLUS 46

Iam ver egelidos refert tepores,
iam caeli furor aequinoctialis
iucundis Zephyri silescit aureis.
linquantur Phrygii, Catulle, campi
5   Nicaeaeque ager uber aestuosae:
ad claras Asiae volemus urbes.
iam mens praetrepidans avet vagari,
iam laeti studio pedes vigescunt.
o dulces comitum valete coetus,
10   longe quos simul a domo profectos
diversae varie viae reportant.

Short Answer Questions

Line 1   What word does *egelidos* modify? _____

Line 2   What word does *aequinoctialis* modify? _____

Line 3   What word does *iucundis* modify? _____

Line 4   What is the mood, tense, and use of *linquantur*? _____

Line 6   What word does *claras* modify? _____

              Translate *volemus*. _____

Line 7   Translate *vagari*. _____

Line 8   What is the case and use of *studio*? _____

Line 9   What is the case and use of *comitum*? _____

Line 10   Translate *profectos*. _____

Multiple Choice Questions *Suggested time: 7 minutes*

1. From lines 1–3, it is clear that
   a. there is a storm brewing
   c. it is too windy to set sail

   b. it is springtime
   d. there is a pleasant silence in the air

2. In line 4, there is an example of
   a. hendiadys
   c. hyperbole

   b. apostrophe
   d. alliteration

3. Line 5 contains an example of
   a. personification
   c. chiasmus

   b. ellipsis
   d. polyptoton

4. From lines 4–8, we learn that
   a. Catullus wants to go to Nicaea
   c. Catullus is not interested in Asia Minor

   b. Catullus is ready to leave Bithynia
   d. Catullus wants to visit Phyrgia

5. In line 9, the word *coetus* refers to
   a. all the places Catullus has seen
   c. Catullus' home

   b. Catullus' sweetheart
   d. Catullus' friends

6. In line 10, the antecedent of *quos* is
   a. *dulces* (line 9)
   c. *coetus* (line 9)

   b. *comitum* (line 9)
   d. *profectos* (line 10)

Translation *Suggested time: 6 minutes*

Translate the passage below as literally as possible.

> **o dulces comitum valete coetus,**
> **longe quos simul a domo profectos**
> **diversae varie viae reportant.**

_____

_____

_____

_____

_____

Short Essay *Suggested time: 20 minutes*

Catullus' happiness pervades Poem 46. Discuss the ways in which Catullus indicates this joy to the reader.

Support your assertions with references drawn from **throughout** the poem. All Latin words must be copied or their line numbers provided, AND they must be translated or paraphrased closely enough so that it is clear you understand the Latin. It is your responsibility to convince your reader that you are basing your conclusions on the Latin text and not merely on a general recollection of the passage. Direct your answer to the question; do not merely summarize the passage. Please write your essay on a separate piece of paper.

Scansion

Scan the following lines and name the meter.

iam caeli furor aequinoctialis

iucundis Zephyri silescit auris.

CATULLUS 49

Disertissime Romuli nepotum,
quot sunt quotque fuere, Marce Tulli,
quotque post aliis erunt in annis,
gratias tibi maximas Catullus
5 **agit pessimus omnium poeta,**
tanto pessimus omnium poeta,
quanto tu optimus omnium patronus.

Short Answer Questions

Line 1   What is the case and degree of *disertissime*? _____

          What is the case and use of *nepotum*? _____

Line 2   What is the alternate form of *fuere*? _____

Line 3   What part of speech is *post* in this sentence? _____

Line 5   What is the case and number of *omnium*? _____

Line 7   What degree is *optimus*? _____

Multiple Choice Questions *Suggested time: 7 minutes*

1. In line 1, *Romuli nepotum* refer to
    a. Cicero's ancestors
    c. Catullus' grandchildren
    b. the Roman people
    d. the six kings after Romulus

2. In lines 2–3, there is an example of
    a. tricolon crescens
    c. hysteron proteron
    b. alliteration
    d. litotes

3. In line 4, *tibi* refers to
    a. Romulus
    c. Catullus
    b. Marcus Tullius
    d. the worst poet

4. From lines 1–5, we learn that

    a. Marcus Tullius idolizes Romulus

    b. the worst poet thinks Romulus is very skilled

    c. there has never been anybody like Romulus

    d. Catullus is thanking Cicero

5. Lines 5–6 contain an example of

    a. synchysis

    b. anaphora

    c. an oxymoron

    d. asyndeton

6. In line 7, *tu* refers to

    a. Cicero

    b. the worst poet

    c. Romulus

    d. Catullus

Translation *Suggested time: 8 minutes*

Translate the passage below as literally as possible.

> **gratias tibi maximas Catullus**
> **agit pessimus omnium poeta,**
> **tanto pessimus omnium poeta,**
> **quanto tu optimus omnium patronus.**

_____

_____

_____

_____

_____

_____

Short Essay *Suggested time: 20 minutes*

Discuss how Catullus' use of superlatives affects the meaning of Poem 49.

Support your assertions with references drawn from **throughout** the poem. All Latin words must be copied or their line numbers provided, AND they must be translated or paraphrased closely enough so that it is clear you understand the Latin. It is your responsibility to convince your reader that you are basing your conclusions on the Latin text and not merely on a general recollection of the passage. Direct your answer to the question; do not merely summarize the passage. Please write your essay on a separate piece of paper.

Scansion

Scan the following lines and name the meter.

quotque post aliis erunt in annis,

gratias tibi maximas Catullus

CATULLUS 50

Hesterno, Licini, die otiosi
multum lusimus in meis tabellis,
ut convenerat esse delicatos:
scribens versiculos uterque nostrum
5   ludebat numero modo hoc modo illoc,
reddens mutua per iocum atque vinum.
atque illinc abii tuo lepore
incensus, Licini, facetiisque,
ut nec me miserum cibus iuvaret
10   nec somnus tegeret quiete ocellos,
sed toto indomitus furore lecto
versarer, cupiens videre lucem,
ut tecum loquerer simulque ut essem.
at defessa labore membra postquam
15   semimortua lectulo iacebant,
hoc, iucunde, tibi poema feci,
ex quo perspiceres meum dolorem.
nunc audax cave sis, precesque nostras,
oramus, cave despuas, ocelle,
20   ne poenas Nemesis reposcat a te.
est vemens dea: laedere hanc caveto.

Short Answer Questions

Line 1   What is the case and use of *Licini?* _____

What is the case and use of *die?* _____

Line 3   Translate *ut convenerat.* _____

Line 4   What does *scribens* modify? _____

What is the case and number of *nostrum?* _____

Line 7   What is the tense, person, and number of *abii?* _____

What is the case and use of *lepore?* _____

Line 9   What type of clause is *ut . . . iuvaret?* _____

Line 10   What is the case and use of *quiete?* _____

Line 11   What is the case and use of *lecto?* _____

Line 12   Translate *versarer.* _____

Line 13   What is the case and use of *te* in the word *tecum?*_____

Line 15   What is the subject of *iacebant?* _____

Line 16   What does *hoc* modify? _____

Line 17   What is the mood and tense of *perspiceres?* _____

Line 18   What grammatical form is *cave?* _____

Line 20   What type of subjunctive clause is *ne . . . te?* _____

Line 21   What grammatical form is *caveto?* _____

Multiple Choice Questions *Suggested time: 10 minutes*

1.   From lines 1–4, we learn that

     a. Licinius was playing a game outside

     b. Licinius and some of his friends had decided to act in an elegant manner

     c. Licinius and Catullus were writing verses together

     d. yesterday Licinius spent a leisurely day alone

2.   In line 5, *numero* refers to

     a. the quantity of verses

     b. how many tablets were available

     c. the meter used

     d. the number of days

3.   In line 7, *tuo* refers to

     a. Licinius

     b. Catullus

     c. one of Licinius' friends

     d. the party atmosphere

4.   From lines 9–11, it is evident that Catullus

     a. is hungry

     b. can't sleep

     c. is angry

     d. can't see

5.   In line 16, *iucunde* refers to

     a. a pleasant poem

     b. Catullus' bed

     c. Licinius

     d. some work

6.   The antecedent of *quo* (line 17) is

     a. *lectulo* (line 15)

     b. *iucunde* (line 16)

     c. *tibi* (line 16)

     d. *poema* (line 16)

7. In lines 18–19, there is an example of

   a. zeugma

   c. chiasmus

   b. alliteration

   d. anaphora

8. In line 21, *hanc* refers to

   a. *dolorem* (line 17)

   c. *ocelle* (line 19)

   b. *preces* (line 18)

   d. *Nemesis* (line 20)

Translation *Suggested time: 6 minutes*

Translate the passage below as literally as possible.

> **scribens versiculos uterque nostrum**
> **ludebat numero modo hoc modo illoc,**
> **reddens mutua per iocum atque vinum.**

_____

_____

_____

_____

_____

Long Essay *Suggested time: 20 minutes*

Poem 50 belongs to a group of poems that address the subject of "what literature can do to you." Discuss the effect that writing poetry appears to have on Catullus.

Support your assertions with references drawn from **throughout** the poem. All Latin words must be copied or their line numbers provided, AND they must be translated or paraphrased closely enough so that it is clear you understand the Latin. It is your responsibility to convince your reader that you are basing your conclusions on the Latin text and not merely on a general recollection of the passage. Direct your answer to the question; do not merely summarize the passage. Please write your essay on a separate piece of paper.

Scansion

Scan the following lines and name the meter.

ut tecum loquerer simulque ut essem.

at defessa labore membra postquam

semimortua lectulo iacebant,

CATULLUS 51

Ille mi par esse deo videtur,
ille, si fas est, superare divos,
qui sedens adversus identidem te
    spectat et audit

5   dulce ridentem, misero quod omnis
eripit sensus mihi: nam simul te,
Lesbia, aspexi, nihil est super mi
    . . .

    lingua sed torpet, tenuis sub artus
10   flamma demanat, sonitu suopte
tintinant aures, gemina teguntur
    lumina nocte.

    otium, Catulle, tibi molestum est:
otio exsultas nimiumque gestis:
15   otium et reges prius et beatas
    perdidit urbes.

Short Answer Questions

Line 1   What is the case of *mi*? _____

                What is the case and use of *deo*? Abl. of ? _____

Line 2   To what verb is *superare* complementary? *divus* _____

Line 3   What is the case, number, and form of *sedens*? pres act participle _____

Line 5   What word does *ridentem* modify? _____

                What word does *misero* modify? _____

Line 6   What is the case and use of *sensus*? _____

Line 7   What is the case and use of *Lesbia*? _____

Line 9   What case is *tenuis,* and what word does it modify? _____

Line 11   What word does *gemina* modify? _____

Line 12   What is the case and use of *nocte*? _____

Line 14   What is the case and use of *Catulle?* _____

Line 15   What is the case and use of *otium?* _____

What word does *beatas* modify? _____

Multiple Choice Questions *Suggested time: 8 minutes*

1. In line 1, *mi* refers to
    a. that man   b. you
    c. Catullus   d. a god

2. The antecedent of *qui* (line 3) is
    a. that man   b. you
    c. Catullus   d. a god

3. From lines 1–4, we learn that
    a. that man can look at you   b. Catullus can hear you
    c. divine beings can conquer you   d. the god is watching over you

4. From lines 5–7, it appears that
    a. Lesbia is miserable   b. that man is laughing
    c. Catullus is overwhelmed   d. you are senseless

5. Lines 9–12 contain an example of
    a. asyndeton   b. hysteron proteron
    c. apostrophe   d. enjambment

6. Lines 13–16 indicate that
    a. kings will destroy cities   b. Catullus bothers some people
    c. leisure is not desirable   d. Lesbia is being too impatient

7. Which of these is **not** present in lines 13–16?
    a. polyptoton   b. anaphora
    c. tricolon crescens   d. synchysis

Translation *Suggested time: 6 minutes*

Translate the passage below as literally as possible.

> **dulce ridentem, misero quod audit omnis**
> **eripit sensus mihi: nam simul te,**
> **Lesbia, aspexi, nihil est super mi**

_____

_____

_____

_____

_____

Long Essay *Suggested time: 30 minutes*

Discuss how references to the senses play an important role in Poem 51.

Support your assertions with references drawn from **throughout** the poem. All Latin words must be copied or their line numbers provided, AND they must be translated or paraphrased closely enough so that it is clear you understand the Latin. It is your responsibility to convince your reader that you are basing your conclusions on the Latin text and not merely on a general recollection of the passage. Direct your answer to the question; do not merely summarize the passage. Please write your essay on a separate piece of paper.

Scansion

Scan the following lines and name the meter.

lingua sed torpet, tenuis sub artus

flamma demanat, sonitu suopte

tintinant aures, gemina teguntur

lumina nocte.

CATULLUS 60

Num te leaena montibus Libystinis
aut Scylla latrans infima inguinum parte
tam mente dura procreavit ac taetra,
ut supplicis vocem in novissimo casu
5   contemptam haberes, a nimis fero corde?

Short Answer Questions

Line 1   What is the case and use of *te*? _____

                What is the case and use of *montibus*? _____

Line 2   What case is *inguinum*? _____

Line 3   What is the case and use of *mente*? _____

Line 5   What does *contemptam* modify? _____

                What is the mood, tense, and use of *haberes*? _____

Multiple Choice Questions *Suggested time: 6 minutes*

1.   In line 1, *num* indicates that the answer to the question will be
    a. brief   b. detailed
    c. negative   d. confusing

2.   In line 2, Scylla is described as a creature
    a. of lowly type   b. who barks
    c. with many parts   d. that is strong

3.   In line 3, *taetra* modifies
    a. *Scylla* (line 2)   b. *parte* (line 2)
    c. *mente* (line 3)   d. *dura* (line 3)

4.   Lines 4–5 contain an example of
    a. an oxymoron   b. hyperbole
    c. hendiadys   d. chiasmus

5. From lines 1–5, we learn that

a. a lion in the African mountains did a monstrous thing

b. a sympathetic voice had been heard

c. the person referred to as *te* did a very cruel thing

d. Scylla surely had a fierce heart

Translation *Suggested time: 10 minutes*

Translate the passage below as literally as possible.

> **Num te leaena montibus Libystinis**
> **aut Scylla latrans infima inguinum parte**
> **tam mente dura procreavit ac taetra,**
> **ut supplicis vocem in novissimo casu**
> **contemptam haberes, a nimis fero corde?**

_____

_____

_____

_____

_____

Short Essay *Suggested time: 20 minutes*

Discuss how the meaning of the word *dura* (line 3) is central to the meaning of Poem 60.

Support your assertions with references drawn from **throughout** the poem. All Latin words must be copied or their line numbers provided, AND they must be translated or paraphrased closely enough so that it is clear you understand the Latin. It is your responsibility to convince your reader that you are basing your conclusions on the Latin text and not merely on a general recollection of the passage. Direct your answer to the question; do not merely summarize the passage. Please write your essay on a separate piece of paper.

Scansion

Scan the following lines and name the meter.

ut supplicis vocem in novissimo casu

contemptam haberes, a nimis fero corde?

REVIEW TWO

Poems 30, 31, 35, 36, 40, 43, 44, 45, 46, 49, 50, 51, 60

Match these people, places, or things to Catullus' description of each.

1.	____ decoctoris amica Formiani	A.	paene insularum . . . insularumque
2.	____ Lesbia	B.	poetae tenero, meo sodali,
3.	____ Acme	C.	immemor atque unanimis false sodalibus,
4.	____ Sirmio	D.	seu Sabine seu Tiburs
5.	____ Alfenus	E.	pleni ruris et inficetiarum . . . , cacata carta
6.	____ Caecilius	F.	dulce ridentem
7.	____ Cicero	G.	hesterno, . . . die otiosi/ multum lusimus
8.	____ O funde noster	H.	leviter caput reflectens/ . . . illo purpureo ore saviata
9.	____ Calvus	I.	nec bello pede nec nigris ocellis
10.	____ Annales Volusi	J.	Disertissime Romuli nepotum

Below are quotations from Catullus' poems. Explain to whom or what the words in bold refer.

1. **ille,** si fas est, superare divos,_____

2. hoc, **iucunde, tibi** poema feci, _____

3. quis **ullos homines beatiores**/ vidit,_____

4. quanto **tu** optimus omnium **patronus.**_____

5. dum in **tuum sinum** fugi,/ et me recuravi _____

6. o dulces **comitum** valete coetus, _____

7. Salve, nec minimo **puella** naso _____

8. at **vos** interea venite in ignem, _____

9. quamvis candida milies **puella**/ euntem revocet, _____

10. scripta **tardipedi deo** daturam _____

Catullus often uses comparative or superlative adjectives in his poetry. Identify whether a comparative or superlative adjective or adverb is present in each quotation below. Then translate the complete line.

1. Sapphica puella musa doctior _____

   _____

2. o quid solutis est beatius curis _____

   _____

3. electissima pessimi poetae scripta _____

   _____

4. ut multo mihi maior acriorque/ ignis _____

   _____

5. in novissimo casu _____

   _____

Long Essay *Suggested time: 30 minutes*

Hesterno, Licini, die otiosi
multum lusimus in meis tabellis,
ut convenerat esse delicatos:
scribens versiculos uterque nostrum
5 ludebat numero modo hoc modo illoc,
reddens mutua per iocum atque vinum.
atque illinc abii tuo lepore
incensus, Licini, facetiisque,
ut nec me miserum cibus iuvaret
10 nec somnus tegeret quiete ocellos,
sed toto indomitus furore lecto
versarer, cupiens videre lucem,
ut tecum loquerer simulque ut essem.
at defessa labore membra postquam
15 semimortua lectulo iacebant,
hoc, iucunde, tibi poema feci,
ex quo perspiceres meum dolorem.
nunc audax cave sis, precesque nostras,
oramus, cave despuas, ocelle,
20 ne poenas Nemesis reposcat a te.
est vemens dea: laedere hanc caveto.

Catullus 50

Ille mi par esse deo videtur,
ille, si fas est, superare divos,
qui sedens adversus identidem te
    spectat et audit
5 dulce ridentem, misero quod omnis
eripit sensus mihi: nam simul te,
Lesbia, aspexi, nihil est super mi
    . . .

lingua sed torpet, tenuis sub artus
10 flamma demanat, sonitu suopte
tintinant aures, gemina teguntur
    lumina nocte.

otium, Catulle, tibi molestum est:
otio exsultas nimiumque gestis:
15 otium et reges prius et beatas
    perdidit urbes.

Catullus 51

Poems 50 and 51 share much of the same language. Identify the verbal parallels that are common to the two poems and discuss their significance for the interpretation of the poems.

Support your assertions with references drawn from **throughout** both poems. All Latin words must be copied or their line numbers provided, AND they must be translated or paraphrased closely enough so that it is clear you understand the Latin. It is your responsibility to convince your reader that you are basing your conclusions on the Latin text and not merely on a general recollection of the passage. Direct your answer to the question; do not merely summarize the passage. Please write your essay on a separate piece of paper.

Scansion

Scan each of the following sets of lines and name the meter for each.

A.

otium, Catulle, tibi molestum est:

otio exsultas nimiumque gestis:

otium et reges prius et beatas

    perdidit urbes.

B.

Quaenam te mala mens, miselle Ravide,

agit praecipitem in meos iambos?

quis deus tibi non bene advocatus

vecordem parat excitare rixam?

CATULLUS 64, LINES 50–75

50   haec vestis priscis hominum variata figuris
        heroum mira virtutes indicat arte.
        namque fluentisono prospectans litore Diae,
        Thesea cedentem celeri cum classe tuetur
        indomitos in corde gerens Ariadna furores,
55   necdum etiam sese quae visit visere credit,
        utpote fallaci quae tum primum excita somno
        desertam in sola miseram se cernat harena.
        immemor at iuvenis fugiens pellit vada remis,
        irrita ventosae linquens promissa procellae.
60   quem procul ex alga maestis Minois ocellis,
        saxea ut effigies bacchantis, prospicit, eheu,
        prospicit et magnis curarum fluctuat undis,
        non flavo retinens subtilem vertice mitram,
        non contecta levi velatum pectus amictu,
65   non tereti strophio lactentis vincta papillas,
        omnia quae toto delapsa e corpore passim
        ipsius ante pedes fluctus salis alludebant.
        sed neque tum mitrae neque tum fluitantis amictus
        illa vicem curans toto ex te pectore, Theseu,
70   toto animo, tota pendebat perdita mente.
        a misera, assiduis quam luctibus externavit
        spinosas Erycina serens in pectore curas,
        illa tempestate, ferox quo ex tempore Theseus
        egressus curvis e litoribus Piraei
75   attigit iniusti regis Gortynia templa.

Short Answer Questions

Line 50   What is the case and use of *vestis?*_____

Line 51   What is the case and number of *heroum?* _____

Line 53   What is the case and use of *Thesea?*_____

             What word modifies *classe?* _____

             Translate *tuetur.* _____

Line 55   What is the grammatical function of the two words *sese . . . visere?*_____

             What is the grammatical function of *quae visit?* _____

Line 56   What word does *fallaci* modify?_____

Line 57   What word does *sola* modify? _____

                     What is the mood of *cernat?* _____

Line 58   What is the case and use of *vada?* _____

Line 59   What is the case and use of *procellae?* _____

Line 60   What is the referent of *quem?* _____

                     What is the case of *Minois?* _____

Line 61   What word does *saxea* modify? _____

                     Translate *ut.* _____

Line 62   Translate *fluctuat.* _____

Line 63   What word does *subtilem* modify? _____

Line 64   Translate *levi,* and identify what word it modifies. _____

                     What is the case and use of *pectus?* _____

Line 65   What is the case and use of *lactentis?* _____

Line 66   What is the case of *omnia quae?* _____

                     Translate *delapsa.* _____

Line 67   What is the case of *fluctus?* _____

Line 69   Translate *vicem.* _____

                     What case is *Theseu?* _____

Line 72   For whom is *Erycina* an epithet? _____

Line 73   What is the case and use of *illa tempestate?* _____

Line 74   Translate *egressus.* _____

Multiple Choice Questions *Suggested time: 11 minutes*

1. What does the coverlet in lines 50–52 show?

    a. the accomplishments of heroes   b. various types of works of art

    c. ancient and amazing symbols   d. the half-man, half-bull monster

2. Lines 52–57 indicate that Ariadne reacts to her abandonment with

    a. resignation   b. fear

    c. excitement   d. disbelief

3. In line 59, there is an example of

    a. polyptoton
    b. hendiadys
    c. chiasmus
    d. synchysis

4. Lines 58–59 indicate that Theseus abandoned Ariadne because

    a. he was cruel
    b. he was in love with someone else
    c. he was forgetful
    d. the other Athenian youths forced him to

5. Which figure of speech is **not** present in lines 63–65?

    a. asyndeton
    b. anaphora
    c. tricolon crescens
    d. anastrophe

6. In line 67, *ipsius* refers to

    a. Theseus
    b. the salty sea
    c. Ariadne
    d. Ariadne's clothes

7. From lines 60–67, we learn that

    a. in her grief Ariadne is acting like a Bacchante
    b. the wind has carried away Ariadne's clothes
    c. Ariadne plans to pursue Theseus
    d. Ariadne is in a state of shock

8. In line 69, there is an example of

    a. a simile
    b. apostrophe
    c. personification
    d. litotes

9. Lines 71–75 reveal that

    a. Ariadne always has been the victim of bad luck
    b. Theseus' family has a long history of perfidious acts
    c. Ariadne's abandonment ultimately is a result of Theseus' earlier arrival on Crete
    d. Venus enjoys pairing lovers who are unsuited to each other

Translation *Suggested time: 6 minutes*

Translate the passage below as literally as possible.

> **necdum etiam sese quae visit visere credit,**
> **utpote fallaci quae tum primum excita somno**
> **desertam in sola miseram se cernat harena.**

_____

_____

_____

_____

_____

Short Essay *Suggested time: 20 minutes*

Discuss how the anaphora in lines 60–70 heightens the pathos of Ariadne's situation.

Support your assertions with references drawn from the passage. All Latin words must be copied or their line numbers provided, AND they must be translated or paraphrased closely enough so that it is clear you understand the Latin. It is your responsibility to convince your reader that you are basing your conclusions on the Latin text and not merely on a general recollection of the passage. Direct your answer to the question; do not merely summarize the passage. Please write your essay on a separate piece of paper.

Long Essay *Suggested time: 30 minutes*

Discuss the importance of perception in Catullus' depiction of Ariadne.

Support your assertions with references drawn from **throughout** these lines. All Latin words must be copied or their line numbers provided, AND they must be translated or paraphrased closely enough so that it is clear you understand the Latin. It is your responsibility to convince your reader that you are basing your conclusions on the Latin text and not merely on a general recollection of the passage. Direct your answer to the question; do not merely summarize the passage. Please write your essay on a separate piece of paper.

Scansion

Scan the following lines and name the meter.

non tereti strophio lactentis vincta papillas,

omnia quae toto delapsa e corpore passim

ipsius ante pedes fluctus salis alludebant.

CATULLUS 64, LINES 76–102

nam perhibent olim crudeli peste coactam
Androgeoneae poenas exsolvere caedis
electos iuvenes simul et decus innuptarum
Cecropiam solitam esse dapem dare Minotauro.
80   quis angusta malis cum moenia vexarentur,
ipse suum Theseus pro caris corpus Athenis
proicere optavit potius quam talia Cretam
funera Cecropiae nec funera portarentur.
atque ita nave levi nitens ac lenibus auris
85   magnanimum ad Minoa venit sedesque superbas.
hunc simul ac cupido conspexit lumine virgo
regia, quam suavis exspirans castus odores
lectulus in molli complexu matris alebat,
quales Eurotae praecingunt flumina myrtus
90   aurave distinctos educit verna colores,
non prius ex illo flagrantia declinavit
lumina, quam cuncto concepit corpore flammam
funditus atque imis exarsit tota medullis.
heu misere exagitans immiti corde furores
95   sancte puer, curis hominum qui gaudia misces,
quaeque regis Golgos quaeque Idalium frondosum,
qualibus incensam iactastis mente puellam
fluctibus, in flavo saepe hospite suspirantem!
quantos illa tulit languenti corde timores!
100   quanto saepe magis fulgore expalluit auri,
cum saevum cupiens contra contendere monstrum
aut mortem appeteret Theseus aut praemia laudis!

Short Answer Questions

Line 76   What word does *coactam* modify? _____

Line 77   To what word does *exsolvere* serve as a complement?_____

Line 78   What is the case and use of *electos iuvenes*? _____

Line 79   What is the case and use of *dapem*? _____

          To what verb does *dare* serve as a complement? _____

Line 80   Give the alternate form of *quis*. _____

What word does *quis* modify? _____

What is the mood and tense of *vexarentur?* _____

Line 81   Translate *suum.* _____

What word does *caris* modify? _____

Line 82   What word does *talia* modify? _____

What is the case and use of *Cretam?* _____

Line 84   What is the case and use of *nave levi* and *lenibus auris*? _____

Line 85   What word does *magnanimum* modify? _____

Line 86   Translate *simul ac.* _____

Line 87   What word does *regia* modify? _____

What word does *suavis* modify? _____

What is the case and use of *odores?* _____

Line 90   Translate *colores.* _____

Line 92   Translate *lumina.* _____

Line 93   What word does *tota* modify? _____

Line 94   What word does *immiti* modify? _____

Line 97   What word does *qualibus* modify? _____

Give the unsyncopated form of *iactastis.* _____

Line 98   What word does *suspirantem* modify? _____

Line 100   What is the case and use of *fulgore?* _____

Line 101   What word does *cupiens* modify? _____

What is the case and use of *monstrum?* _____

Line 102   What is the mood and tense of *appeteret?* _____

Multiple Choice Questions *Suggested time: 12 minutes*

1. In line 76, the subject of *perhibent* is
   a. chosen youths
   c. Androgeos
   b. the flower of maidens
   d. an unspecified "they"

2. In lines 76–79, which statement is **not** true?
   a. Athens has been visited by a cruel disease
   c. Athenian youths had to pay a penalty for the death of Androgeos
   b. Athenian youths attended a banquet in Crete every seventh year
   d. Athenian youths provided food for the Minotaur

3. Line 81, contains an example of
   a. asyndeton
   c. metonymy
   b. homoteletuton
   d. synchysis

4. In line 86, *hunc* refers to
   a. Theseus
   c. the Minotaur
   b. Minos
   d. Androgeos

5. The subject of *alebat* (line 88) is
   a. *odores* (line 87)
   c. *complexu* (line 88)
   b. *lectulus* (line 88)
   d. *matris* (line 88)

6. Lines 89–93 do **not** contain an example of
   a. alliteration
   c. personification
   b. a simile
   d. tmesis

7. Which of the following words in lines 91–93 does not refer to burning?
   a. *flagrantia* (line 91)
   c. *flammam* (line 92)
   b. *concepit* (line 92)
   d. *exarsit* (line 93)

8. In line 94, *misere* is a(n)
   a. syncopated third person plural verb, perfect tense, active voice
   c. imperative in the passive voice
   b. infinitive
   d. adverb

9. In lines 94–98, the poet addresses
   a. Theseus
   c. Cupid and Venus
   b. Androgeos
   d. Venus

10. Lines 100–102 describe
    a. Ariadne's fear for Theseus' safety
    b. the cruelty of the Minotaur
    c. Ariadne's love for Theseus
    d. Theseus fighting the Minotaur with his sword

Translation *Suggested time: 6 minutes*

Translate the passage below as literally as possible.

> quanto saepe magis fulgore expalluit auri,
> cum saevum cupiens contra contendere monstrum
> aut mortem appeteret Theseus aut praemia laudis!

_____

_____

_____

_____

_____

_____

Long Essay *Suggested time: 30 minutes*

Discuss how the metaphors in lines 91–102 enhance the meaning of these lines.

Support your assertions with references drawn from the passage. All Latin words must be copied or their line numbers provided, AND they must be translated or paraphrased closely enough so that it is clear you understand the Latin. It is your responsibility to convince your reader that you are basing your conclusions on the Latin text and not merely on a general recollection of the passage. Direct your answer to the question; do not merely summarize the passage. Please write your essay on a separate piece of paper.

Scansion

Scan the following lines and name the meter.

electos iuvenes simul et decus innuptarum

Cecropiam solitam esse dapem dare Minotauro.

quis angusta malis cum moenia vexarentur,

CATULLUS 64, LINES 103–131

  non ingrata tamen frustra munuscula divis
  promittens tacito succepit vota labello.
105 nam velut in summo quatientem bracchia Tauro
  quercum aut conigeram sudanti cortice pinum
  indomitus turbo contorquens flamine robur,
  eruit (illa procul radicitus exturbata
  prona cadit, late quaevis cumque obvia frangens),
110 sic domito saevum prostravit corpore Theseus
  nequiquam vanis iactantem cornua ventis.
  inde pedem sospes multa cum laude reflexit
  errabunda regens tenui vestigia filo,
  ne labyrintheis e flexibus egredientem
115 tecti frustraretur inobservabilis error.
    sed quid ego a primo digressus carmine plura
  commemorem, ut linquens genitoris filia vultum,
  ut consanguineae complexum, ut denique matris,
  quae misera in gnata deperdita laeta<batur>,
120 omnibus his Thesei dulcem praeoptarit amorem:
  aut ut vecta rati spumosa ad litora Diae
  <venerit,> aut ut eam devinctam lumina somno
   liquerit immemori discedens pectore coniunx?
  saepe illam perhibent ardenti corde furentem
125 clarisonas imo fudisse e pectore voces,
  ac tum praeruptos tristem conscendere montes,
  unde aciem <in> pelagi vastos protenderet aestus,
  tum tremuli salis adversas procurrere in undas
  mollia nudatae tollentem tegmina surae,
130 atque haec extremis maestam dixisse querellis,
  frigidulos udo singultus ore cientem:

Short Answer Questions

Line 103   What word does *ingrata* modify? _____

Line 104   What is the object of *succepit*? _____

Line 105   What word does *quatientem* modify? _____

Line 106   What is the case and use of *sudanti cortice*? _____

Line 107   What is the case and use of *turbo?* _____

                Translate *robur.* _____

                What is its case and use? _____

Line 108   What are the direct objects of *eruit?* _____

                To which word does *illa* refer? _____

                What part of speech is *radicitus?* _____

Line 109   What is the case and use of *obvia?* _____

Line 110   What is the case and use of the two words d*omito . . . corpore?* _____

Line 111   What word does *vanis* modify? _____

                What word does *iactatem* modify? _____

Line 112   What is the case and use of *sospes?* _____

Line 113   What word does *tenui* modify? _____

Line 114   What is the case and use of *egredientem?* _____

Line 115   What is the subject of *frustraretur?* _____

                What is its mood and tense? _____

Line 116   Translate *quid.* _____

Line 117   What is the mood and use of *commemorem?* _____

                Translate *ut.* _____

Line 119   What is the antecedent of *quae?* _____

                What word does *deperdita* modify? _____

Line 120   What is the unsyncopated form of *praeoptarit?* _____

Line 121   Translate *vecta.* _____

                What is the case and use of *rati?* _____

Line 122   What is the case and use of *lumina?* _____

Line 123   To whom does *coniunx* refer? _____

Line 124   To whom does *illam* refer? _____

                What is its case and use? _____

Line 125   What word modifies *voces?* _____

                What degree is *imo?* _____

Line 126   What is the case and use of *tristem?* _____

Line 127   Translate *aciem.* _____

                   What is the case and use of *pelagi?* _____

                   What mood and tense is *protenderet?* _____

Line 129   What word does *mollia* modify? _____

                   What word does *tollentem* modify? _____

Line 130   What is the case and use of *maestam?* _____

                   What is the case and use of *haec?* _____

Line 131   What is the case and use of *singultus?* _____

Multiple Choice Questions *Suggested time: 8 minutes*

1.   In line 103, there is an example of

     a. anaphora   b. hyperbole

     c. litotes   d. hendiadys

2.   Regarding the content of lines 105–111, which statement is true?

     a. the trunk of a pine and oak tree is uprooted   b. a bull is caught up in a whirlwind and dies

     c. a whirlwind causes Theseus to fall headlong   d. Theseus overcomes the savage Minotaur

3.   In lines 114–115, *ne* introduces a(n)

     a. negative purpose clause   b. negative result clause

     c. deliberative subjunctive   d. indirect question

4.   Lines 117–118 do **not** contain an example of

     a. an oxymoron   b. tricolon crescens

     c. alliteration   d. anaphora

5.   Which statement is **not** true about the content of lines 116–123?

     a. Ariadne considered Theseus her spouse   b. Ariadne's father was delighted that she was in love with Theseus

     c. Ariadne preferred Theseus over her immediate family   d. Ariadne sailed with Theseus to the shores of Dia

6. In lines 116–120, *ut* introduces a(n)

    a. purpose clause
    b. result clause
    c. deliberative subjunctive
    d. indirect question

7. Which statement does **not** accurately reflect Ariadne's reaction to Theseus' departure in lines 124–131?

    a. she is angry
    b. she is sad
    c. she is frantic
    d. she is suicidal

Translation *Suggested time: 8 minutes*

Translate the passage below as literally as possible.

> inde pedem sospes multa cum laude reflexit
> errabunda regens tenui vestigia filo,
> ne labyrintheis e flexibus egredientem
> tecti frustraretur inobservabilis error.

_____

_____

_____

_____

_____

_____

_____

Short Essay *Suggested time: 20 minutes*

Describe how the simile in lines 105–109 anticipates and enhances the description of Theseus' heroic deed in lines 110–111.

Support your assertions with references drawn from the passage. All Latin words must be copied or their line numbers provided, AND they must be translated or paraphrased closely enough so that it is clear you understand the Latin. It is your responsibility to convince your reader that you are basing your conclusions on the Latin text and not merely on a general recollection of the passage. Direct your answer to the question; do not merely summarize the passage. Please write your essay on a separate piece of paper.

Long Essay *Suggested time: 30 minutes*

In lines 116–131, Catullus juxtaposes Ariadne's preference for her lover over her immediate family to Theseus' abandonment of her. What reaction to Ariadne's situation does the language in these lines elicit?

Support your assertions with references drawn from these lines. All Latin words must be copied or their line numbers provided, AND they must be translated or paraphrased closely enough so that it is clear you understand the Latin. It is your responsibility to convince your reader that you are basing your conclusions on the Latin text and not merely on a general recollection of the passage. Direct your answer to the question; do not merely summarize the passage. Please write your essay on a separate piece of paper.

Scansion

Scan the following lines and name the meter.

errabunda regens tenui vestigia filo,

ne labyrintheis e flexibus egredientem

tecti frustraretur inobservabilis error.

CATULLUS 64, LINES 132–157

"sicine me patriis avectam, perfide, ab aris,
perfide, deserto liquisti in litore, Theseu?
sicine discedens neglecto numine divum,
135   immemor a! devota domum periuria portas?
nullane res potuit crudelis flectere mentis
consilium? tibi nulla fuit clementia praesto,
immite ut nostri vellet miserescere pectus?
at non haec quondam blanda promissa dedisti
140   voce mihi, non haec miserae sperare iubebas,
sed conubia laeta, sed optatos hymenaeos,
quae cuncta aerii discerpunt irrita venti.
nunc iam nulla viro iuranti femina credat,
nulla viri speret sermones esse fideles;
145   quis dum aliquid cupiens animus praegestit apisci,
nil metuunt iurare, nihil promittere parcunt:
sed simul ac cupidae mentis satiata libido est,
dicta nihil metuere, nihil periuria curant.
certe ego te in medio versantem turbine leti
150   eripui, et potius germanum amittere crevi,
quam tibi fallaci supremo in tempore dessem.
pro quo dilaceranda feris dabor alitibusque
praeda, neque iniacta tumulabor mortua terra.
quaenam te genuit sola sub rupe leaena,
155   quod mare conceptum spumantibus exspuit undis,
quae Syrtis, quae Scylla rapax, quae vasta Carybdis,
talia qui reddis pro dulci praemia vita?

Short Answer Questions

Line 132   What word does *perfide* modify? _____

Line 134   What is the case and use of *numine*? _____

                  Give the case and number of *divum*. _____

Line 135   What is the case and use of *domum*? _____

Line 136   What word does *crudelis* modify? _____

Line 137   What is the case and use of *tibi*? _____

Line 138   What word does *immite* modify? _____

What is the mood and tense of *vellet*? _____

What is the case and use of *nostri*? _____

Line 143   What is the case and use of *viro*? _____

Line 145   Give the alternate form of *quis*. _____

Line 147   Translate *simul ac*. _____

Line 148   What is subject of *metuere*? _____

Line 151   What is the case and use of *tibi*? _____

What word does *fallaci* modify? _____

Line 152   What part of speech is *dilaceranda*? _____

Line 153   What does *mortua* modify? _____

What is the case and use of *terra*? _____

Line 154   What word does *sola* modify? _____

Line 155   What is the case and use of *undis*? _____

Line 157   What word does *dulci* modify? _____

Multiple Choice Questions *Suggested time: 6 minutes*

1.   Lines 132–35 do **not** contain an example of

    a. anaphora   b. chiasmus

    c. apostrophe   d. litotes

2.   In lines 139–40, *blanda* modifies

    a. *haec* (line 139)   b. *promissa* (line 139)

    c. *voce* (line 140)   d. *mihi* (line 140)

3.   In lines 143–144, which of the following is true?

    a. *speret* is a deliberative subjunctive   b. *viro* is dative after the special verb *credo*

    c. *sermones* is a nominative plural subject   d. *iuranti* is a participle modifying *femina*

4. What does Ariadne **not** mention in lines 149–151?

   a. the gods forced her to choose Theseus over her brother

   b. she rescued Theseus from death

   c. in saving Theseus, she lost a brother

   d. her decision to help Theseus was deliberate

5. Lines 154–156 do **not** contain an example of

   a. ellipsis

   b. tricolon crescens

   c. polysyndeton

   d. anaphora

Translation *Suggested time: 10 minutes*

Translate the passage below as literally as possible.

> quaenam te genuit sola sub rupe leaena,
> quod mare conceptum spumantibus exspuit undis,
> quae Syrtis, quae Scylla rapax, quae vasta Carybdis,
> talia qui reddis pro dulci praemia vita?

_____

_____

_____

_____

_____

_____

Short Essay *Suggested time: 20 minutes*

How do Ariadne's questions to the absent Theseus in lines 132–138 enhance her lament?

Support your assertions with references drawn from the passage. All Latin words must be copied or their line numbers provided, AND they must be translated or paraphrased closely enough so that it is clear you understand the Latin. It is your responsibility to convince your reader that you are basing your conclusions on the Latin text and not merely on a general recollection of the passage. Direct your answer to the question; do not merely summarize the passage. Please write your essay on a separate piece of paper.

Scansion

Scan the following lines and name the meter.

certe ego te in medio versantem turbine leti

eripui, et potius germanum amittere crevi

quam tibi fallaci supremo in tempore dessem.

CATULLUS 64, LINES 158–187

si tibi non cordi fuerant conubia nostra,
saeva quod horrebas prisci praecepta parentis,
160 attamen in vestras potuisti ducere sedes,
quae tibi iucundo famularer serva labore,
candida permulcens liquidis vestigia lymphis,
purpureave tuum consternens veste cubile.
sed quid ego ignaris nequiquam conquerar auris,
165 externata malo, quae nullis sensibus auctae
nec missas audire queunt nec reddere voces?
ille autem prope iam mediis versatur in undis,
nec quisquam apparet vacua mortalis in alga.
sic nimis insultans extremo tempore saeva
170 fors etiam nostris invidit questibus auris.
Iuppiter omnipotens, utinam ne tempore primo
Cnosia Cecropiae tetigissent litora puppes,
indomito nec dira ferens stipendia tauro
perfidus in Cretam religasset navita funem,
175 nec malus hic celans dulci crudelia forma
consilia in nostris requiesset sedibus hospes!
nam quo me referam? quali spe perdita nitor?
Idaeosne petam montes? at gurgite lato
discernens ponti truculentum dividit aequor.
180 an patris auxilium sperem? quemne ipsa reliqui
respersum iuvenem fraterna caede secuta?
coniugis an fido consoler memet amore?
quine fugit lentos incurvans gurgite remos?
praeterea nullo colitur sola insula tecto,
185 nec patet egressus pelagi cingentibus undis.
nulla fugae ratio, nulla spes: omnia muta,
omnia sunt deserta, ostentant omnia letum.

Short Answer Questions

Line 158   What is the use of *tibi?* _____

Line 159   What word does *saeva* modify? _____

Line 161   What is the understood antecedent of *quae?* _____

          What is the mood and tense of *famularer?* _____

          What is the case and use of *serva?* _____

Line 162   Translate *vestigia.* _____

             What is the case and use of *lymphis?* _____

Line 163   What word does *purpurea* modify? _____

Line 164   What is the case of *auris?* _____

Line 165   What word does *externata* modify? _____

             What word does *auctae* modify? _____

Line 166   What word does *missas* modify? _____

Line 167   Translate *versatur.* _____

Line 168   What is the case and use of *mortalis?* _____

Line 171   What is the case and use of *Iuppiter?* _____

Line 172   What word does *Cecropiae* modify? _____

             What is the mood and tense of *tetigissent?* _____

Line 173   What word does *indomito* modify? _____

Line 174   What word does *perfidus* modify? _____

             Give the unsyncopated form of *religasset.* _____

Line 175   What word does *dulci* modify? _____

             What is the case and number of *crudelia?* _____

Line 176   Give the unsyncopated form of *requiesset.* _____

Line 177   What is the case and use of *spe?* _____

Line 179   What is the case and use of *aequor?* _____

Line 180   What is the antecedent of *quem?* _____

Line 181   What word does *secuta* modify? _____

Line 182   What is the case and use of *coniugis?* _____

             What is the non-emphatic form of *memet?* _____

Line 184   Translate *sola.* _____

             What is the case and use of *tecto?* _____

Line 185   What is the case and use of *undis?* _____

Line 187   What is the case and use of *letum?* _____

Multiple Choice Questions *Suggested time: 13 minutes*

1. In line 161, the verb *famularer* is in a(n)

   a. result clause

   c. indirect question

   b. deliberative question

   d. relative clause of purpose

2. In line 162, there is an example of

   a. alliteration

   c. personification

   b. synchysis

   d. chiasmus

3. From lines 158–163, we learn that

   a. Ariadne desires to be queen of Athens

   c. Ariadne fears Theseus' father

   b. Ariadne would be willing to be Theseus' slave

   d. Ariadne would settle for a platonic relationship with Theseus

4. Line 163 is a(n)

   a. hypermetric line

   c. golden line

   b. spondaic line

   d. chiastic line

5. In line 164, the verb *conquerar* is in a(n)

   a. deliberative question

   c. indirect command

   b. indirect question

   d. relative clause of purpose

6. In line 166, there is an example of

   a. hendiadys

   c. hyperbole

   b. alliteration

   d. chiasmus

7. The case of *auris* in line 170 is

   a. genitive

   c. accusative

   b. nominative

   d. ablative

8. In line 171 there is an example of

   a. an oxymoron

   c. apostrophe

   b. tmesis

   d. anaphora

9. The subject of *requiesset* in line 176 is

   a. *hic* (line 175)

   c. *consilia* (line 176)

   b. *forma* (line 175)

   d. *hospes* (line 176)

10. The verb *referam* in line 177 is in a(n)

    a. deliberative question

    b. indirect question

    c. indirect command

    d. optative subjunctive expressing wish

11. The subject of *dividit* in line 179 is

    a. *gurgite* (line 178)

    b. *ponti* (line 179)

    c. *truculentum* (line 179)

    d. *aequor* (line 179)

12. In line 185, what part of speech is the word *egressus*?

    a. adverb

    b. participle

    c. noun

    d. adjective

Translation *Suggested time: 6 minutes*

Translate the passage below as literally as possible.

> **nam quo me referam? quali spe perdita nitor?**
> **Idaeosne petam montes? at gurgite lato**
> **discernens ponti truculentum dividit aequor.**

_____

_____

_____

_____

_____

Short Essay *Suggested time: 20 minutes*

Discuss how Catullus frames this passage with references to home and family (lines 158–163; 180–182) and thus enhances the theme of Ariadne's utter abandonment.

Support your assertions with references drawn from **throughout** the passage. All Latin words must be copied or their line numbers provided, AND they must be translated or paraphrased closely enough so that it is clear you understand the Latin. It is your responsibility to convince your reader that you are basing your conclusions on the Latin text and not merely on a general recollection of the passage. Direct your answer to the question; do not merely summarize the passage. Please write your essay on a separate piece of paper.

Scansion

Scan the following lines and name the meter.

nec patet egressus pelagi cingentibus undis.

nulla fugae ratio, nulla spes: omnia muta,

omnia sunt deserta, ostentant omnia letum.

CATULLUS 64, LINES 188–227

non tamen ante mihi languescent lumina morte,
nec prius a fesso secedent corpore sensus,
190   quam iustam a divis exposcam prodita multam
caelestumque fidem postrema comprecer hora.
quare facta virum multantes vindice poena
Eumenides, quibus anguino redimita capillo
frons exspirantis praeportat pectoris iras,
195   huc huc adventate, meas audite querellas,
quas ego, vae misera, extremis proferre medullis
cogor inops, ardens, amenti caeca furore.
quae quoniam verae nascuntur pectore ab imo,
vos nolite pati nostrum vanescere luctum,
200   sed quali solam Theseus me mente reliquit,
tali mente, deae, funestet seque suosque."
    has postquam maesto profudit pectore voces,
supplicium saevis exposcens anxia factis,
annuit invicto caelestum numine rector;
205   quo motu tellus atque horrida contremuerunt
aequora concussitque micantia sidera mundus.
ipse autem caeca mentem caligine Theseus
consitus oblito dimisit pectore cuncta,
quae mandata prius constanti mente tenebat,
210   dulcia nec maesto sustollens signa parenti
sospitem Erectheum se ostendit visere portum.
namque ferunt olim, classi cum moenia divae
linquentem gnatum ventis concrederet Aegeus,
talia complexum iuveni mandata dedisse:
215   "gnate mihi longa iucundior unice vita,
gnate, ego quem in dubios cogar dimittere casus,
reddite in extrema nuper mihi fine senectae,
quandoquidem fortuna mea ac tua fervida virtus
eripit invito mihi te, cui languida nondum
220   lumina sunt gnati cara saturata figura,
non ego te gaudens laetanti pectore mittam,
nec te ferre sinam fortunae signa secundae,
sed primum multas expromam mente querellas,
canitiem terra atque infuso pulvere foedans,
225   inde infecta vago suspendam lintea malo,
nostros ut luctus nostraeque incendia mentis
carbasus obscurata dicet ferrugine Hibera.

Short Answer Questions

Line 188   What is the case and use of *mihi?* _____

              What is the case and use of *morte?* _____

Line 189   What word does *fesso* modify? _____

Line 190   What case is *prodita* and what does it modify? _____

              What is the case and use of *multam?* _____

Line 191   What is the case and use of *caelestum?* _____

Line 192   What is the case and use of *virum?* _____

Line 193   What is the case and use of *Eumenides?* _____

              What case is *redimita,* and what does it modify? _____

Line 194   What case is *exspirantis,* and what does it modify? _____

Line 196   What form is *proferre,* and what is its use? _____

Line 197   What word does *amenti* modify? _____

Line 199   Translate *nolite pati.* _____

              What is the case and use of *luctum?* _____

Line 201   What is the mood and tense of *funestet?* _____

Line 202   What word does *has* modify? _____

Line 203   What does *anxia* modify? _____

Line 204   What is the case and use of *numine?* _____

Line 206   What is the case and use of *sidera?* _____

Line 207   What is the case and use of *caligine?* _____

Line 210   What does *dulcia* modify? _____

Line 211   What does *sospitem* modify? _____

Line 212   Translate *ferunt.* _____

              What is the case and use of *classi?* _____

Line 214   What is the case and use of *talia?* _____

              What does *complexum* modify? _____

Line 215   What is the case and use of *vita?* _____

Line 216   What is the antecedent of *quem?* _____

            What word does *dubios* modify? _____

Line 217   What does *extrema* modify? _____

Line 219   What is the case and use of *mihi?* _____

Line 220   What is the case and use of *figura?* _____

Line 221   What is the case and use of *laetanti?* _____

Line 224   What is the case and use of *infuso?* _____

Line 225   Translate *malo.* _____

Line 227   What is the case and use of *obscurata?* _____

            Translate *dicet.* _____

            What is the case and use of *ferrugine?* _____

Multiple Choice Questions *Suggested time: 18 minutes*

1. Lines 189–190 contain an example of

    a. anaphora   b. hyperbole

    c. litotes   d. tmesis

2. In lines 188–191, which statement is **not** true?

    a. Ariadne thinks she is going to die   b. Ariadne is weary

    c. Ariadne expects that Theseus will return   d. Ariadne asks the gods for a just penalty

3. In line 193, *capillo* is an ablative of

    a. means   b. cause

    c. manner   d. separation

4. In line 197, there is an example of

    a. anastrophe   b. tricolon crescens

    c. metonymy   d. anaphora

5. In line 198, the antecedent of *quae* is

    a. *querellas* (line 195)   b. *ego* (line 196)

    c. *medullis* (line 196)   d. *furore* (line 197)

6. In line 199, *vanescere* is

    a. a complementary infinitive   b. an infinitive with subject accusative

    c. present, passive, second person, singular   d. third person, plural, perfect indicative

7. Line 201 contains an example of

    a. asyndeton

    c. hyperbole

    b. apostrophe

    d. anaphora

8. In line 205, *quo motu* is an ablative of

    a. cause

    c. comparison

    b. agent

    d. accompaniment

9. Line 207 contains an example of

    a. chiasmus

    c. assonance

    b. synchysis

    d. tmesis

10. In line 211, the accusative subject of *visere* is

    a. *signa* (line 210)

    c. *Erectheum* (line 211)

    b. *parenti* (line 210)

    d. *se* (line 211)

11. In line 212, *divae* refers to

    a. Hera

    c. Athena

    b. Aphrodite

    d. Artemis

12. The case of *ventis* (line 213) is

    a. genitive

    c. accusative

    b. dative

    d. ablative

13. In line 217, *reddite* is

    a. present tense, plural, imperative

    c. masculine, singular, participle, vocative

    b. an adverb of the first and second declension

    d. future tense, plural, imperative

14. In line 226, *ut* introduces a

    a. clause of fearing

    c. temporal clause

    b. purpose clause

    d. result clause

15. In lines 215–227, which of the following statements is **not** true about Aegeus?

    a. he hangs black sails on the mast of his son's ship

    c. he grieves for his son who is on the point of departing

    b. he curses Fortune for restoring his son to him so late in his life

    d. he values his son more than he values a long life for himself

Translation *Suggested time: 6 minutes*

Translate the passage below as literally as possible.

> namque ferunt olim, classi cum moenia divae
> linquentem gnatum ventis concrederet Aegeus,
> talia complexum iuveni mandata dedisse:

_____

_____

_____

_____

Long Essay *Suggested time: 30 minutes*

Discuss how the themes of loss of family, forgetfulness, and betrayal are interwoven in this passage.

Support your assertions with references drawn from **throughout** the passage. All Latin words must be copied or their line numbers provided, AND they must be translated or paraphrased closely enough so that it is clear you understand the Latin. It is your responsibility to convince your reader that you are basing your conclusions on the Latin text and not merely on a general recollection of the passage. Direct your answer to the question; do not merely summarize the passage. Please write your essay on a separate piece of paper.

Scansion

Scan the following lines and name the meter.

vos nolite pati nostrum vanescere luctum,

sed quali solam Theseus me mente reliquit,

tali mente, deae, funestet seque suosque.

CATULLUS 64, LINES 228-253

      quod tibi si sancti concesserit incola Itoni,
      quae nostrum genus ac sedes defendere Erecthei
230   annuit, ut tauri respergas sanguine dextram,
      tum vero facito ut memori tibi condita corde
      haec vigeant mandata, nec ulla oblitteret aetas;
      ut simul ac nostros invisent lumina collis,
      funestam antennae deponant undique vestem,
235   candidaque intorti sustollant vela rudentes,
      quam primum cernens ut laeta gaudia mente
      agnoscam, cum te reducem aetas prospera sistet."
      haec mandata prius constanti mente tenentem
      Thesea ceu pulsae ventorum flamine nubes
240   aereum nivei montis liquere cacumen.
      at pater, ut summa prospectum ex arce petebat,
      anxia in assiduos absumens lumina fletus,
      cum primum infecti conspexit lintea veli,
      praecipitem sese scopulorum e vertice iecit,
245   amissum credens immiti Thesea fato.
      sic funesta domus ingressus tecta paterna
      morte ferox Theseus, qualem Minoidi luctum
      obtulerat mente immemori, talem ipse recepit.
      quae tum prospectans cedentem maesta carinam
250   multiplices animo volvebat saucia curas.
          at parte ex alia florens volitabat Iacchus
      cum thiaso Satyrorum et Nysigenis Silenis,
      te quaerens, Ariadna, tuoque incensus amore.

Short Answer Questions

Line 228   Translate *quod.*_____

Line 229   What is the antecedent of *quae?* _____

Line 230   What is the case and use of *sanguine?* _____

Line 231   What does *memori* modify?_____

Line 233   Translate *simul ac.* _____

            What is the case and use of *collis?* _____

Line 234   What does *funestam* modify? _____

Line 235   What does *intorti* modify?_____

Line 236   Translate *quam primum*. _____

                What is the case and use of *mente*? _____

Line 237   What is the mood and tense of *sistet?* _____

Line 238   What is the case and use of *mandata?* _____

                What word does *tenentem* modify? _____

Line 239   What is the case and use of *flamine?* _____

                What word does *pulsae* modify? _____

Line 241   Translate *ut*. _____

                What word does *summa* modify? _____

Line 242   What word does *assiduos* modify? _____

Line 244   What is the case and use of *sese?* _____

Line 245   What is the case and use of *fato?* _____

Line 246   What word does *funesta* modify? _____

                What is the case and use of *domus?* _____

Line 247   What is the case and use of *morte?* _____

Line 249   What does *maesta* modify? _____

Line 250   What word does *multiplices* modify? _____

Line 251   What word does *alia* modify? _____

Line 253   Translate *tuo amore*. _____

Multiple Choice Questions *Suggested time: 11 minutes*

1. In line 230, *ut* introduces a
    a. substantive result clause
    b. clause of fearing
    c. substantive purpose clause
    d. temporal clause

2. The use of *facito* (line 231) is a(an)
    a. ablative of means
    b. dative of separation
    c. adverb
    d. future imperative

3. In line 236, *laeta* is modifying
    a. *vela* (line 235)
    b. *gaudia* (line 236)
    c. *mente* (line 236)
    d. *aetas* (line 237)

4. Lines 238–40 contain an example of

   a. a simile

   b. metaphor

   c. synchysis

   d. onomatopoeia

5. In line 240, *liquere* is

   a. an infinitive

   b. an imperative

   c. passive, future tense, second person singular

   d. third person, plural, perfect tense indicative

6. What does **not** happen in lines 238–245?

   a. Theseus forgets his father's earlier instructions

   b. Aegeus believes Theseus is dead

   c. Aegeus throws himself off the cliff

   d. the clouds obscure Theseus' view of land

7. In line 246, *paterna* is modifying

   a. *domus* (line 246)

   b. *tecta* (line 246)

   c. *morte* (line 247)

   d. *Minoidi* (line 247)

8. In 249, the antecedent of *quae* is

   a. *morte* (line 247)

   b. *Minoidi* (line 247)

   c. *luctum* (line 247)

   d. *mente* (line 248)

9. In line 250, *animo* is a(n)

   a. dative of reference

   b. dative of agent

   c. ablative of place where

   d. ablative of means

Translation *Suggested time: 6 minutes*

Translate the passage below as literally as possible.

> sic funesta domus ingressus tecta paterna
> morte ferox Theseus, qualem Minoidi luctum
> obtulerat mente immemori, talem ipse recepit.

_____

_____

_____

_____

_____

Long Essay *Suggested time: 30 minutes*

Discuss how repetition of language related to perception and memory interconnects Ariadne, Aegeus, and Theseus in this passage.

Support your assertions with references drawn from **throughout** the passage. All Latin words must be copied or their line numbers provided, AND they must be translated or paraphrased closely enough so that it is clear you understand the Latin. It is your responsibility to convince your reader that you are basing your conclusions on the Latin text and not merely on a general recollection of the passage. Direct your answer to the question; do not merely summarize the passage. Please write your essay on a separate piece of paper.

Scansion

Scan the following lines and name the meter.

at pater, ut summa prospectum ex arce petebat,

anxia in assiduos absumens lumina fletus,

cum primum infecti conspexit lintea veli,

CATULLUS 65

Etsi me assiduo confectum cura dolore
    sevocat a doctis, Hortale, virginibus,
nec potis est dulcis Musarum expromere fetus
    mens animi, tantis fluctuat ipsa malis—
5   namque mei nuper Lethaeo gurgite fratris
    pallidulum manans alluit unda pedem,
Troia Rhoeteo quem subter litore tellus
    ereptum nostris obterit ex oculis.

. . . .

10   numquam ego te, vita frater amabilior,
aspiciam posthac? at certe semper amabo,
    semper maesta tua carmina morte canam,
qualia sub densis ramorum concinit umbris
    Daulias, absumpti fata gemens Ityli.—
15   sed tamen in tantis maeroribus, Hortale, mitto
    haec expressa tibi carmina Battiadae,
ne tua dicta vagis nequiquam credita ventis
    effluxisse meo forte putes animo,
ut missum sponsi furtivo munere malum
20   procurrit casto virginis e gremio,
quod miserae oblitae molli sub veste locatum,
    dum adventu matris prosilit, excutitur,
atque illud prono praeceps agitur decursu,
    huic manat tristi conscius ore rubor.

Short Answer Questions

Line 1   What word does *confectum* modify? _____

            What is the case and use of *dolore?* _____

Line 2   What is the direct object of *sevocat?* _____

Line 3   What word does *dulcis* modify, and what case is it? _____

Line 4   What is the case and use of *malis?* _____

Line 5   What is the case and use of *gurgite?* _____

Line 7   What word does *Troia* modify? _____

Line 8   What word does *ereptum* modify? _____

Line 10   What is the case and use of *vita?* _____

Line 12   What is the case and use of *morte*? _____

Line 13   What word is the subject of *concinit?* _____

Line 14   What word does *gemens* modify?_____

Line 16   What is the case of *Battiadae?* _____

Line 17   What is the case and use of *ventis?* _____

Line 18   What is the mood and tense of *putes?* _____

               What is the case and use of *animo?* _____

Line 21   What word does *molli* modify?_____

Line 23   What word does *praeceps* modify? _____

Line 24   What word does *conscius* modify? _____

Multiple Choice Questions *Suggested time: 19 minutes*

1.   Line 1 contains an example of
     a.   synchysis   b.   hyperbole
     c.   an oxymoron   d.   polyptoton

2.   In line 4, *ipsa* refers to
     a.   one of the Muses   b.   a girlfriend
     c.   Catullus' mind   d.   Catullus' concern

3.   Line 6 contains an example of
     a.   synchysis   b.   a transferred epithet
     c.   tmesis   d.   chiasmus

4.   In line 7, the antecedent of *quem* is
     a.   *gurgite* (line 5)   b.   *fratris* (line 5)
     c.   *pedem* (line 6)   d.   *tellus* (line 7)

5.   From lines 1–7, it is clear that
     a.   Hortalus has sent Catullus a letter   b.   Catullus' brother is on the shore of Troy
          expressing sorrow at the loss of his
          brother
     c.   Catullus is mourning the death of his   d.   Catullus' mind is pouring forth poems
          brother   about the death of his brother

6. In line 10, *te* refers to
   a. Hortalus
   b. Catullus
   c. Catullus' brother
   d. Daulias

7. The death of Catullus' brother in lines 11–14 is compared to
   a. the death of Daulias
   b. the fate of Itylus
   c. the poems of Battiades
   d. the sadness Catullus feels

8. In line 18, *putes* is in a negative
   a. result clause
   b. indirect command
   c. purpose clause
   d. indirect question

9. From lines 15–18, we learn that
   a. Catullus did what Hortalus has asked
   b. Hortalus translated some poems
   c. Hortalus forgot about Callimachus' poems
   d. Catullus was grieving too much to do anything

10. In line 19, *ut* means
    a. so that
    b. in order to
    c. how
    d. as

11. In line 21, *quod* refers to
    a. *munere* (line 19)
    b. *malum* (line 19)
    c. *gremio* (line 20)
    d. *locatum* (line 21)

12. *oblitae* (line 21) refers to
    a. *sponsi* (line 19)
    b. *virginis* (line 20)
    c. *veste* (line 21)
    d. *matris* (line 22)

13. In line 23, *illud* refers to
    a. *malum* (line 19)
    b. *gremio* (line 20)
    c. *adventu* (line 22)
    d. *decursu* (line 23)

14. Line 23 contains an example of
    a. chiasmus
    b. synchysis
    c. polysyndeton
    d. personification

15. The scansion of the first four feet of line 23 is
    a. spondee, dactyl, spondee, spondee
    b. dactyl, spondee, spondee, dactyl
    c. dactyl, dactyl, spondee, spondee
    d. spondee, spondee, spondee, dactyl

16. From lines 19–24, we learn that

   a. the mother did not want the girl to have the apple

   b. the apple was a secret gift from the girl's boyfriend

   c. the girl was sad because her mother disliked her boyfriend

   d. when the girl found the apple in her lap, she blushed

Translation *Suggested time: 8 minutes*

Translate the passage below as literally as possible.

> namque mei nuper Lethaeo gurgite fratris
> pallidulum manans alluit unda pedem,
> Troia Rhoeteo quem subter litore tellus
> ereptum nostris obterit ex oculis.

_____

_____

_____

_____

_____

_____

Long Essay *Suggested time: 30 minutes*

Discuss how the final simile in Poem 65 (lines 19–24) links Catullus and the *virgo* through the themes of forgetfulness and embarrassment.

Support your assertions with references drawn from the poem. All Latin words must be copied or their line numbers provided, AND they must be translated or paraphrased closely enough so that it is clear you understand the Latin. It is your responsibility to convince your reader that you are basing your conclusions on the Latin text and not merely on a general recollection of the passage. Direct your answer to the question; do not merely summarize the passage. Please write your essay on a separate piece of paper.

Scansion

Scan the following lines and name the meter.

ut missum sponsi furtivo munere malum

procurrit casto virginis e gremio,

CATULLUS 68

Quod mihi fortuna casuque oppressus acerbo
    conscriptum hoc lacrimis mittis epistolium,
naufragum ut eiectum spumantibus aequoris undis
    sublevem et a mortis limine restituam,
5   quem neque sancta Venus molli requiescere somno
    desertum in lecto caelibe perpetitur,
nec veterum dulci scriptorum carmine Musae
    oblectant, cum mens anxia pervigilat:
id gratum est mihi, me quoniam tibi dicis amicum,
10   muneraque et Musarum hinc petis et Veneris.
sed tibi ne mea sint ignota incommoda, Manli,
    neu me odisse putes hospitis officium,
accipe, quis merser fortunae fluctibus ipse,
    ne amplius a misero dona beata petas.
15   tempore quo primum vestis mihi tradita pura est,
    iucundum cum aetas florida ver ageret,
multa satis lusi: non est dea nescia nostri,
    quae dulcem curis miscet amaritiem.
sed totum hoc studium luctu fraterna mihi mors
20   abstulit. o misero frater adempte mihi,
tu mea tu moriens fregisti commoda, frater,
    tecum una tota est nostra sepulta domus,
omnia tecum una perierunt gaudia nostra,
    quae tuus in vita dulcis alebat amor.
25   cuius ego interitu tota de mente fugavi
    haec studia atque omnes delicias animi.
quare, quod scribis Veronae turpe Catullo
    esse, quod hic quisquis de meliore nota
frigida deserto tepefactet membra cubili,
30   id, Manli, non est turpe, magis miserum est.
ignosces igitur si, quae mihi luctus ademit,
    haec tibi non tribuo munera, cum nequeo.
nam, quod scriptorum non magna est copia apud me,
    hoc fit, quod Romae vivimus: illa domus,
35   illa mihi sedes, illic mea carpitur aetas;
    huc una ex multis capsula me sequitur.
quod cum ita sit, nolim statuas nos mente maligna
    id facere aut animo non satis ingenuo,
quod tibi non utriusque petenti copia posta est:
40   ultro ego deferrem, copia siqua foret.

Short Answer Questions

Line 1   What is the case and use of *fortuna?* _____

                   What word does *acerbo* modify? _____

Line 2   What word does *hoc* modify? _____

                   What is the case and use of *lacrimis?* _____

Line 4   What is the mood and tense of *sublevem?* _____

Line 5   What word does *molli* modify? _____

Line 7   What word modifies *carmine?* _____

                   What is the case and use of *Musae?* _____

Line 9   What is the case and use of *me?* _____

Line 11   What is the case and use of *tibi?* _____

                   What is the case and use of *Manli?* _____

Line 12   What is the tense and use of *odisse?* _____

Line 13   What case is *quis?* _____

Line 14   What is the mood and tense of *petas?* _____

Line 15   What is the case and use of *tempore?* _____

                   What word does *pura* modify? _____

Line 16   What word does *florida* modify? _____

                   What is the mood and tense of *ageret?* _____

Line 17   What is the case and use of *multa?* _____

Line 19   What is the case and use of *luctu?* _____

Line 20   What is the case and use of *mihi?* _____

Line 22   What word does *tota* modify? _____

Line 24   What word does *dulcis* modify? _____

Line 26   What word does *haec* modify? _____

Line 27   Translate *quod.* _____

                   What case is *Veronae?* _____

                   What gender is *turpe?* _____

Line 28   What is the form and use of *esse?* _____

Line 29   What word does *deserto* modify? _____

Line 32   What is the case and use of *tibi*? _____

Line 34   Translate *quod.* _____

Line 35   What is the case and use of *mihi*? _____

Line 37   What is the mood and tense of *statuas*? _____

Line 38   What is the case and use of *animo*? _____

Line 39   What word does *petenti* modify? _____

            What is the unsyncopated form of *posta*? _____

Line 40   What is the alternate form of *foret*? _____

Multiple Choice Questions *Suggested time: 25 minutes*

1. To whom does the subject of *mittis* (line 2) refer?

    a. *fortuna* (line 1)   b. *conscriptum* (line 2)
    c. *Venus* (line 5)   d. *Manli* (line 11)

2. In line 3, *naufragum* refers to

    a. Manlius   b. Venus
    c. Catullus   d. one of the Muses

3. Line 3 contains an example of

    a. synchysis   b. metaphor
    c. personification   d. hendiadys

4. In line 4, *restituam* is

    a. a future active indicative   b. a volitive subjunctive
    c. a subjunctive verb in a purpose clause   d. an accusative singular

5. The antecedent of *quem* (line 5) is

    a. *epistolium* (line 2)   b. *naufragum* (line 3)
    c. *aequoris* (line 3)   d. *limine* (line 4)

6. From lines 1–8, we learn that

    a. Catullus is distraught over the death of his brother   b. Manlius has suffered a major misfortune and is unable to sleep
    c. Venus cannot seem to fall asleep   d. the songs of the Muses no longer delight Catullus

7. In line 9, *id* refers to
   a. Manlius' request
   c. holy Venus
   b. the song of the Muses
   d. pleasant sleep

8. Line 11 contains a
   a. negative result clause
   c. negative indirect command
   b. positive fear clause
   d. negative purpose clause

9. The subject of *merser* (line 13) refers to
   a. Manlius
   c. Catullus
   b. a Muse
   d. Venus

10. Line 16 contains an example of
    a. chiasmus
    c. a transferred epithet
    b. synchysis
    d. a simile

11. In line 17, there is an example of
    a. apostrophe
    c. anastrophe
    b. litotes
    d. an oxymoron

12. The antecedent of *quae* (line 18) is
    a. *aetas* (line 16)
    c. *dea* (line 17)
    b. *multa* (line 17)
    d. *amaritiem* (line 18)

13. In line 20, there is an example of
    a. personification
    c. apostrophe
    b. hysteron proteron
    d. synecdoche

14. From lines 9–20, we learn that
    a. a goddess has avenged herself on Manlius
    c. Manlius has broken the bonds of the guest-host relationship
    b. Catullus cannot do what Manlius has asked of him
    d. it is spring and the time for love

15. In line 23, *te* in *tecum* refers to
    a. Manlius
    c. Catullus' brother
    b. Catullus
    d. Venus

16. The antecedent of *quae* (line 24) is
    a. *sepulta* (line 22)
    c. *vita* (line 24)
    b. *gaudia* (line 23)
    d. *amor* (line 24)

17. Line 29 contains an example of

    a. hyperbole   b. irony

    c. synchysis   d. metonymy

18. In line 37, *nolim* is a subjunctive verb in a(n)

    a. potential sentence   b. cum clause

    c. purpose clause   d. indirect question

19. In line 38, *facere* is a(n)

    a. complementary infinitive   b. objective infinitive

    c. infinitive in indirect discourse   d. infinitive with an impersonal verb

20. In line 40, *deferrem* is an imperfect subjunctive in a(n)

    a. present contrary to fact condition   b. purpose clause

    c. optative wish   d. indirect command

21. From lines 27–40, we learn that

    a. Catullus does not have many of his   b. Manlius thinks it is disgraceful that
       writings with him in Verona   Catullus is in Rome

    c. Catullus thinks Manlius has acted out   d. Manlius wants to send a gift to Catullus
       of evil intentions   in Verona

Translation *Suggested time: 10 minutes*

Translate the passage below as literally as possible.

> quare, quod scribis Veronae turpe Catullo
>   esse, quod hic quisquis de meliore nota
> frigida deserto tepefactet membra cubili,
>   id, Manli, non est turpe, magis miserum est.

_____

_____

_____

_____

_____

_____

Long Essay *Suggested time: 30 minutes*

In Poem 68 Manlius has lost the ability to enjoy poetry while Catullus has lost the ability to create poetry. Discuss how these themes of love, loss, and poetry integrate this poem.

Support your assertions with references drawn from **throughout** the poem. All Latin words must be copied or their line numbers provided, AND they must be translated or paraphrased closely enough so that it is clear you understand the Latin. It is your responsibility to convince your reader that you are basing your conclusions on the Latin text and not merely on a general recollection of the passage. Direct your answer to the question; do not merely summarize the passage. Please write your essay on a separate piece of paper.

Scansion

Scan the following lines and name the meter.

quod cum ita sit, nolim statuas nos mente maligna

id facere aut animo non satis ingenuo,

REVIEW THREE

Poems 64, lines 50–253; 65; 68

Match the figure of speech to the line that exemplifies it.

1. _____ alliteration

2. _____ transferred epithet

3. _____ synchysis

4. _____ tmesis

5. _____ apostrophe

6. _____ tricolon crescens

7. _____ simile

8. _____ litotes

A. illa vicem curans toto ex te pectore, Theseu

B. omnia muta,/ omnia sunt deserta, ostentant omnia letum.,

C. nec veterum dulci scriptorum carmine

D. sed tibi ne mea sint ignota incommoda, Manli

E. qualia sub densis ramorum concinit umbris

F. Thesea cedentem celeri cum classe tuetur

G. nec prius a fesso secedent corpore sensus,/ quam . . .

H. desertum in lecto caelibe perpetitur

Below are quotations from Catullus' poems 64, 65, and 68. Explain to whom or what the words in bold refer.

1. haec expressa tibi carmina **Battiadae** _____

2. **vestis** mihi tradita pura est, _____

3. haec **vestis** priscis hominum variata figuris _____

4. Cecropiam solitam esse **dapem** dare Minotauro. _____

5. hunc simul ac cupido conspexit lumine **virgo** _____

6. haec **tibi** non tribuo munera, cum nequeo. _____

7. sancte **puer,** curis hominum qui gaudia misces, _____

8. quaenam **te** genuit sola sub rupe leaena _____

9. ut linquens **genitoris** filia vultum _____

10. quod tibi non utriusque petenti **copia** posta est: _____

Catullus is fond of using diminutives in his poetry. Identify which word is the diminutive in each line and explain what effect it has on the meaning of the line.

1. lectulus in molli complexu matris alebat

   _____

   _____

   _____

2. conscriptum hoc lacrimis mittis epistolium

   _____

   _____

   _____

3. non ingrata tamen frustra munuscula divis

   _____

   _____

   _____

4. frigidulos udo singultus ore cientem

   _____

   _____

   _____

Long Essay *Suggested time: 30 minutes*

Alfene immemor atque unanimis false sodalibus,
iam te nil miseret, dure, tui dulcis amiculi?
iam me prodere, iam non dubitas fallere, perfide?
nec facta impia fallacum hominum caelicolis placent.
5 quae tu neglegis ac me miserum deseris in malis.
eheu quid faciant, dic, homines cuive habeant fidem?
certe tute iubebas animam tradere, inique, <me>
inducens in amorem, quasi tuta omnia mi forent.
idem nunc retrahis te ac tua dicta omnia factaque
10 ventos irrita ferre ac nebulas aereas sinis.
si tu oblitus es, at di meminerunt, meminit Fides,
quae te ut paeniteat postmodo facti faciet tui.

Catullus 30

"sicine me patriis avectam, perfide, ab aris,
perfide, deserto liquisti in litore, Theseu?
sicine discedens neglecto numine divum,
135 immemor a! devota domum periuria portas?
nullane res potuit crudelis flectere mentis
consilium? tibi nulla fuit clementia praesto,
immite ut nostri uellet miserescere pectus?
at non haec quondam blanda promissa dedisti
140 voce mihi, non haec miserae sperare iubebas,
sed conubia laeta, sed optatos hymenaeos,
quae cuncta aerii discerpunt irrita venti.
nunc iam nulla viro iuranti femina credat,
nulla viri speret sermones esse fideles;
145 quis dum aliquid cupiens animus praegestit apisci,
nil metuunt iurare, nihil promittere parcunt:
sed simul ac cupidae mentis satiata libido est,
dicta nihil metuere, nihil periuria curant.

Catullus 64: 132–148

Discuss how the language in Ariadne's lament in lines 132–148 of Poem 64 recalls the language of betrayal in Poem 30 and indicate the significance of this verbal interplay for understanding the values that Catullus especially espouses.

Support your assertions with references drawn from **throughout** both poems. All Latin words must be copied or their line numbers provided, AND they must be translated or paraphrased closely enough so that it is clear you understand the Latin. It is your responsibility to convince your reader that you are basing your conclusions on the Latin text and not merely on a general recollection of the passage. Direct your answer to the question; do not merely summarize the passage. Please write your essay on a separate piece of paper.

Scansion

Scan each of the following sets of lines and name the meter for each.

A.

ut simul ac nostros invisent lumina collis,

funestam antennae deponant undique vestem,

candidaque intorti sustollant vela rudentes,

quam primum cernens ut laeta gaudia mente

B.

cuius ego interitu tota de mente fugavi

    haec studia atque omnes delicias animi.

quare, quod scribis Veronae turpe Catullo

    esse, quod hic quisquis de meliore nota

CATULLUS 69

Noli admirari, quare tibi femina nulla,
    Rufe, velit tenerum supposuisse femur,
non si illam rarae labefactes munere vestis
    aut perluciduli deliciis lapidis.
5   laedit te quaedam mala fabula, qua tibi fertur
    valle sub alarum trux habitare caper.
hunc metuunt omnes, neque mirum: nam mala valde est
    bestia, nec quicum bella puella cubet.
quare aut crudelem nasorum interfice pestem,
10   aut admirari desine cur fugiunt.

Short Answer Questions

Line 1   What form is *admirari?* _____

             What is the case and use of *tibi?* _____

Line 2   What is the case and use of *Rufe?* _____

Line 3   What is the case and use of *munere?* _____

Line 4   What word does *perluciduli* modify? _____

Line 5   Translate *fertur.* _____

             What word does *quaedam* modify? _____

Line 6   What word is the object of *sub?* _____

Line 8   What is the mood, tense, and voice of *cubet?* _____

Line 9   What grammatical form is *interfice?* _____

Line 10   Translate *admirari.* _____

Multiple Choice Questions *Suggested time: 12 minutes*

1.   In line 1, *quare* means

    a. who

                           b. why

    c. ask

                           d. therefore

2. In line 2,
    a. *velit* is a present subjunctive in an indirect question
    b. *supposuisse* is a perfect passive infinitive depending on *velit*
    c. *tenerum* modifies the word "man" understood
    d. *femur* is the neuter nominative subject of the clause

3. From lines 1–2, we learn that
    a. the girls admire Rufus
    b. Rufus likes to look at the girls' legs
    c. the girls do not like to be with Rufus
    d. Rufus does not like the girls

4. In line 3, *illam* refers to
    a. a translucent stone
    b. the dress
    c. a girl
    d. the delightful gift

5. In line 3, *rarae* modifies
    a. *illam*
    b. *labefactes*
    c. *munere*
    d. *vestis*

6. *te* (line 5) refers to
    a. Rufus
    b. a girl
    c. Catullus
    d. the goat

7. In line 6, *trux* modifies
    a. *valle*
    b. *alarum*
    c. the understood subject
    d. *caper*

8. Line 6 contains an example of
    a. anastrophe
    b. synchysis
    c. synecdoche
    d. hendiadys

9. From lines 5–8, we learn that
    a. Rufus got hurt by a savage beast
    b. there was a story being told about a goat with wings
    c. Rufus' armpits emit a nasty odor
    d. the savage beast will not live in a valley

10. In lines 9–10, there is/are
    a. one enjambment
    b. two elisions
    c. one synizesis
    d. two diaereses

Translation *Suggested time: 4 minutes*

Translate the passage below as literally as possible.

non si illam rarae labefactes munere vestis
aut perluciduli deliciis lapidis.

_____

_____

_____

_____

Long Essay *Suggested time: 30 minutes*

Discuss how Poem 69 is integrated thematically through the image of the goat with its various symbolic associations.

Support your assertions with references drawn from **throughout** the poem. All Latin words must be copied or their line numbers provided, AND they must be translated or paraphrased closely enough so that it is clear you understand the Latin. It is your responsibility to convince your reader that you are basing your conclusions on the Latin text and not merely on a general recollection of the passage. Direct your answer to the question; do not merely summarize the passage. Please write your essay on a separate piece of paper.

Scansion

Scan the following lines and name the meter.

quare aut crudelem nasorum interfice pestem,

aut admirari desine cur fugiunt.

CATULLUS 70

Nulli se dicit mulier mea nubere malle
    quam mihi, non si se Iuppiter ipse petat.
dicit: sed mulier cupido quod dicit amanti,
    in vento et rapida scribere oportet aqua.

Short Answer Questions

Line 1   What is the case and use of *nulli*? _____

          What is the case and use of *se*? _____

          What form is *malle*? _____

Line 2   What is the mood, tense, voice, and use of *petat*? _____

          Translate *quam*. _____

Line 3   What word does *cupido* modify? _____

Line 4   What is the case and use of *aqua*? _____

Multiple Choice Questions *Suggested time: 6 minutes*

1. In line 2, *mihi* refers to
    a. the woman   b. Jupiter
    c. Catullus   d. nobody

2. According to lines 1–2,
    a. Jupiter asks the woman to marry him   b. nobody wants to marry the woman
    c. the woman says she wants to marry *"mihi"*   d. the woman prefers to marry Jupiter

3. In line 3,
    a. *quod* means "because"   b. *mulier* is the subject of *dicit* in the *quod* clause
    c. *amanti* is the subject of the *quod* clause   d. *cupido* is the antecedent of *quod*

4. Lines 1–3 contain an example of
    a. zeugma   b. metonymy
    c. anaphora   d. onomatopoeia

5. In line 4, *in vento et rapida . . . aqua* describe something that

    a. will cause a storm at sea

    b. Jupiter can control

    c. will not be permanent

    d. the woman wants to look at

Translation *Suggested time: 4 minutes*

Translate the passage below as literally as possible.

Nulli se dicit mulier mea nubere malle
quam mihi, non si se Iuppiter ipse petat.

_____

_____

_____

Short Essay *Suggested time: 20 minutes*

Discuss how the imagery in line 4 affects or enhances the meaning of Poem 70.

Support your assertions with references drawn from **throughout** the poem. All Latin words must be copied or their line numbers provided, AND they must be translated or paraphrased closely enough so that it is clear you understand the Latin. It is your responsibility to convince your reader that you are basing your conclusions on the Latin text and not merely on a general recollection of the passage. Direct your answer to the question; do not merely summarize the passage. Please write your essay on a separate piece of paper.

Scansion

Mark the scansion of the following lines.

dicit: sed mulier cupido quod dicit amanti,

in vento et rapida scribere oportet aqua.

CATULLUS 72

Dicebas quondam solum te nosse Catullum,
Lesbia, nec prae me velle tenere Iovem.
dilexi tum te non tantum ut vulgus amicam,
sed pater ut gnatos diligit et generos.
5   nunc te cognovi: quare, etsi impensius uror,
multo mi tamen es vilior et levior.
qui potis est, inquis? quod amantem iniuria talis
cogit amare magis, sed bene velle minus.

Short Answer Questions

Line 1   What is the case and use of *te*?_____

Translate *solum.*_____

What is the unsyncopated form of *nosse?*_____

Line 2   What case is *Lesbia?* _____

What is the case and use of *me?* _____

Line 3   Translate *ut.*_____

Line 5   What part of speech and form is *impensius?* _____

Line 6   What is the case and use of *multo?* _____

Line 7   What word does *talis* modify? _____

Multiple Choice Questions *Suggested time: 5 minutes*

1. In line 1, *te* refers to
   a. Catullus
   c. Jupiter
   b. Lesbia
   d. the common people

2. From lines 1–2, we learn that
   a. Catullus used to love Lesbia
   c. Lesbia used to hold Jupiter
   b. Lesbia used to prefer Catullus
   d. Catullus used to talk about Lesbia

3. In line 3, there is an example of

   a. synchysis

   b. alliteration

   c. hyperbaton

   d. metonymy

4. Line 4 contains an example of a(n)

   a. simile

   b. chiasmus

   c. apostrophe

   d. tricolon crescens

5. From lines 5–6, we learn that

   a. Catullus has just come to know Lesbia

   b. Lesbia now seems cheap to Catullus

   c. Catullus is exceedingly angry with himself

   d. Lesbia is being very gentle towards Catullus

Translation *Suggested time: 4 minutes*

Translate the passage below as literally as possible.

dilexi tum te non tantum ut vulgus amicam,
sed pater ut gnatos diligit et generos.

_____

_____

_____

_____

Long Essay *Suggested time: 30 minutes*

Discuss the ways in which Catullus depicts his relationship with Lesbia in this poem.

Support your assertions with references drawn from **throughout** the poem. All Latin words must be copied or their line numbers provided, AND they must be translated or paraphrased closely enough so that it is clear you understand the Latin. It is your responsibility to convince your reader that you are basing your conclusions on the Latin text and not merely on a general recollection of the passage. Direct your answer to the question; do not merely summarize the passage. Please write your essay on a separate piece of paper.

Scansion

Scan the following lines and name the meter.

nunc te cognovi: quare, etsi impensius uror,

multo mi tamen es vilior et levior.

CATULLUS 76

Siqua recordanti benefacta priora voluptas
    est homini, cum se cogitat esse pium,
nec sanctam violasse fidem, nec foedere nullo
    divum ad fallendos numine abusum homines,
5   multa parata manent in longa aetate, Catulle,
    ex hoc ingrato gaudia amore tibi.
nam quaecumque homines bene cuiquam aut dicere possunt
    aut facere, haec a te dictaque factaque sunt.
omnia quae ingratae perierunt credita menti.
10   quare iam te cur amplius excrucies?
quin tu animo offirmas atque istinc teque reducis,
    et dis invitis desinis esse miser?
difficile est longum subito deponere amorem,
    difficile est, verum hoc qua lubet efficias:
15   una salus haec est, hoc est tibi pervincendum,
    hoc facias, sive id non pote sive pote.
o di, si vestrum est misereri, aut si quibus umquam
    extremam iam ipsa in morte tulistis opem,
me miserum aspicite et, si vitam puriter egi,
20   eripite hanc pestem perniciemque mihi,
quae mihi subrepens imos ut torpor in artus
    expulit ex omni pectore laetitias.
non iam illud quaero, contra me ut diligat illa,
    aut, quod non potis est, esse pudica velit:
25   ipse valere opto et taetrum hunc deponere morbum.
    o di, reddite mi hoc pro pietate mea.

Short Answer Questions

Line 1   What is the case and grammatical form of *recordanti?* _____

Line 2   What is the case and use of *homini?* _____

        What is the case and use of *se?* _____

Line 3   What is the unsyncopated form, tense, and voice of *violasse?* _____

Line 4   What is the grammatical form of *fallendos,* and what is its use? _____

        What is the case and use of *numine?* _____

Line 5   What word does *multa* modify? _____

Line 7   What is the case and use of *quaecumque*? _____

Line 8   What is the case and use of *te?* _____

Line 9   What word does *ingratae* modify? _____

Line 10   What tense is *excrucies?* _____

Line 12   What is the case and use of *dis?* _____

Line 14   Translate *verum*. _____

Line 15   What is the case and use of *tibi?* _____

              What construction is *est . . . pervincendum?* _____

Line 16   What is the mood, tense, and use of *facias?* _____

Line 17   What case is *di?* _____

Line 18   What word does *ipsa* modify? _____

Line 20   What is the case and use of *mihi?* _____

Line 21   What word does *imos* modify? _____

Line 23   What part of speech is *contra?* _____

Line 24   What is the mood and tense of *velit?* _____

Line 26   What is the case and use of *mi?* _____

Multiple Choice Questions *Suggested time: 12 minutes*

1. In lines 1–2, there is an example of
   a. metonymy   b. chiasmus
   c. hyperbole   d. apostrophe

2. According to lines 1–6, Catullus expects
   a. happiness because he has been a good   b. retribution because he has deceived
      and loyal person   certain individuals
   c. a long life because he has worshipped   d. a joyful reunion with the one he loves
      the gods

3. From lines 7–12, we learn that
   a. human beings cannot seem to do things   b. all things are dying
      the right way
   c. Lesbia is torturing Catullus   d. Catullus does not want to be miserable
                                                     anymore

4. In lines 13–14, the anaphora emphasizes
   a. the sudden occurrence of this event
   b. how pleasing it is
   c. the long duration of love
   d. the difficulty of the task

5. In line 16, *hoc* refers to
   a. defeating the impossible
   b. doing what is pleasing
   c. putting aside love
   d. achieving what is possible

6. The gods are described, in lines 17–18, as able to
   a. offer help
   b. pity her
   c. go to the extreme
   d. bring death

7. In line 20, there is an example of
   a. chiasmus
   b. polysyndeton
   c. metaphor
   d. litotes

8. According to lines 19–22, Catullus' love for Lesbia is **not** described as
   a. a disease
   b. what made him unhappy
   c. something that crept slowly into his life
   d. a numbness in his limbs

9. In line 23, *illud* refers to
   a. his former happiness
   b. the disease
   c. Lesbia's love for him
   d. his heart

10. In lines 25–26,
    a. the gods recognize Catullus' loyalty
    b. Catullus asks to become loyal
    c. Catullus prays to be released from loving Lesbia
    d. the gods return happiness to Catullus

Translation *Suggested time: 15 minutes*

Translate the passage below as literally as possible.

> una salus haec est, hoc est tibi pervincendum,
>> hoc facias, sive id non pote sive pote.
> o di, si vestrum est misereri, aut si quibus umquam
>> extremam iam ipsa in morte tulistis opem,
> 5   me miserum aspicite et, si vitam puriter egi,
>> eripite hanc pestem perniciemque mihi,
> quae mihi subrepens imos ut torpor in artus
>> expulit ex omni pectore laetitias.

_____

_____

_____

_____

_____

_____

_____

_____

_____

_____

_____

_____

Long Essay *Suggested time: 30 minutes*

Miser Catulle, desinas ineptire,
et quod vides perisse perditum ducas.
fulsere quondam candidi tibi soles,
cum ventitabas quo puella ducebat
5   amata nobis quantum amabitur nulla.
ibi illa multa cum iocosa fiebant,
quae tu volebas nec puella nolebat,
fulsere vere candidi tibi soles.
nunc iam illa non volt: tu quoque inpote<ns noli>,
10   nec quae fugit sectare, nec miser vive,
sed obstinata mente prefer, obdura.
vale, puella. iam Catullus obdurat,
nec te requiret nec rogabit invitam.
at tu dolebis, cum rogaberis nulla.
15   scelesta, vae te, quae tibi manet vita?
quis nunc te adibit? cui videberis bella?
quem nunc amabis? cuius esse diceris?
quem basiabis? cui labella mordebis?
at tu, Catulle, destinatus obdura.

Catullus 8

Siqua recordanti benefacta priora voluptas
  est homini, cum se cogitat esse pium,
nec sanctam violasse fidem, nec foedere nullo
  divum ad fallendos numine abusum homines,
5 multa parata manent in longa aetate, Catulle,
  ex hoc ingrato gaudia amore tibi.
nam quaecumque homines bene cuiquam aut dicere possunt
  aut facere, haec a te dictaque factaque sunt.
omnia quae ingratae perierunt credita menti.
10   quare iam te cur amplius excrucies?
quin tu animo offirmas atque istinc teque reducis,
  et dis invitis desinis esse miser?
difficile est longum subito deponere amorem,
  difficile est, verum hoc qua lubet efficias:
15 una salus haec est, hoc est tibi pervincendum,
  hoc facias, sive id non pote sive pote.
o di, si vestrum est misereri, aut si quibus umquam
  extremam iam ipsa in morte tulistis opem,
me miserum aspicite et, si vitam puriter egi,
20   eripite hanc pestem perniciemque mihi,
quae mihi subrepens imos ut torpor in artus
  expulit ex omni pectore laetitias.
non iam illud quaero, contra me ut diligat illa,
  aut, quod non potis est, esse pudica velit:
25 ipse valere opto et taetrum hunc deponere morbum.
  o di, reddite mi hoc pro pietate mea.

Catullus 76

Poems 8 and 76 are self-reflective pieces in which Catullus attempts to persuade himself that his relationship with Lesbia is over. Compare and contrast his treatment of this similar theme in the two poems.

Support your assertions with references drawn from **throughout** both poems. All Latin words must be copied or their line numbers provided, AND they must be translated or paraphrased closely enough so that it is clear you understand the Latin. It is your responsibility to convince your reader that you are basing your conclusions on the Latin text and not merely on a general recollection of the passage. Direct your answer to the question; do not merely summarize the passage. Please write your essay on a separate piece of paper.

Scansion

Scan the following lines and name the meter.

nam quaecumque homines bene cuiquam aut dicere possunt

aut facere, haec a te dictaque factaque sunt.

CATULLUS 77

Rufe mihi frustra ac nequiquam credite amice
    (frustra? immo magno cum pretio atque malo),
sicine subrepsti mi, atque intestina perurens
    ei misero eripuisti omnia nostra bona?
5   eripuisti, heu heu nostrae crudele venenum
    vitae, heu heu nostrae pestis amicitiae.

Short Answer Questions

Line 1   What is the case and use of *Rufe?* _____

Line 2   What is the case and use of *pretio?* _____

Line 3   What is the unsyncopated form of *subrepsti?* _____

            What word does *perurens* modify? _____

Line 4   Translate *ei.* _____

            What word does *misero* modify? _____

Line 5   What is the case and use of *venenum?* _____

Multiple Choice Questions *Suggested time: 6 minutes*

1.   In line 1, *credite* is a(n)

    a. plural imperative   b. perfect passive participle

    c. noun in the vocative   d. adverb

2.   Line 1 contains an example of

    a. irony   b. hysteron proteron

    c. pleonasm   d. synecdoche

3.   In line 3, there is an example of

    a. synchysis   b. alliteration

    c. hyperbaton   d. metonymy

4.   In line 4, *omnia nostra bona* refer to

    a.   Lesbia's love for Catullus

    b.   the good times Catullus and Rufus had together

    c.   Rufus' and Catullus' joint property holdings

    d.   Catullus' love of life

5.   In lines 5–6, there is an example of

    a.   chiasmus

    b.   hendiadys

    c.   apostrophe

    d.   tmesis

Translation *Suggested time: 4 minutes*

Translate the passage below as literally as possible.

> **sicine subrepsti mi, atque intestina perurens**
> **ei misero eripuisti omnia nostra bona?**

_____

_____

_____

Short Essay *Suggested time: 20 minutes*

Discuss how the use of anaphora emphasizes the emotion that Catullus is expressing in Poem 77.

Support your assertions with references drawn from **throughout** the poem. All Latin words must be copied or their line numbers provided, AND they must be translated or paraphrased closely enough so that it is clear you understand the Latin. It is your responsibility to convince your reader that you are basing your conclusions on the Latin text and not merely on a general recollection of the passage. Direct your answer to the question; do not merely summarize the passage. Please write your essay on a separate piece of paper.

Long Essay *Suggested time: 30 minutes*

This poem contains subtle allusions to Catullus' love affair with Lesbia. Identify and discuss those allusions.

Support your assertions with references drawn from **throughout** the poem. All Latin words must be copied or their line numbers provided, AND they must be translated or paraphrased closely enough so that it is clear you understand the Latin. It is your responsibility to convince your reader that you are basing your conclusions on the Latin text and not merely on a general recollection of the passage. Direct your answer to the question; do not merely summarize the passage. Please write your essay on a separate piece of paper.

Scansion

Scan the following lines and name the meter.

Rufe mihi frustra ac nequiquam credite amice

(frustra? immo magno cum pretio atque malo),

CATULLUS 84

Chommoda dicebat, si quando commoda vellet
    dicere, et insidias Arrius hinsidias,
et tum mirifice sperabat se esse locutum,
    cum quantum poterat dixerat hinsidias.
5   credo, sic mater, sic liber avunculus eius,
    sic maternus avus dixerat atque avia.
hoc misso in Syriam requierant omnibus aures:
    audibant eadem haec leniter et leviter,
nec sibi postilla metuebant talia verba,
10   cum subito affertur nuntius horribilis,
Ionios fluctus, postquam illuc Arrius isset,
    iam non Ionios esse sed Hionios.

Short Answer Questions

Line 1   What is the subject of *dicebat*?_____

                 What is the mood and tense of *vellet*? _____

Line 3   What is the case and use of *se*? _____

Line 4   Translate *cum.* _____

Line 5   What word does *liber* modify? _____

Line 7   What is the case and use of *hoc*? _____

Line 8   What grammatical form is *leniter*?_____

Line 9   Translate *postilla.*_____

Line 10   What word does *horribilis* modify? _____

Line 11   What is the case and use of *fluctus*?_____

                 What is the mood and tense of *isset?*_____

Multiple Choice Questions *Suggested time: 12 minutes*

1. In line 2, *dicere* is
   a. an infinitive in indirect statement
   b. the subject of the *si* clause
   c. complementary to *vellet*
   d. the alternate form of *diceris*

2. Line 2 contains an example of
   a. synchysis
   b. ellipsis
   c. synizesis
   d. zeugma

3. Lines 1–2 (*Chommoda . . . dicere*) contain an example of
   a. polyptoton
   b. hendiadys
   c. an oxymoron
   d. anastrophe

4. From lines 1–4, we learn that Arrius
   a. used to talk too much
   b. often mispronounced words
   c. hoped to learn to speak better
   d. wanted opportunities

5. In line 7, *omnibus* is a dative of
   a. agent
   b. reference
   c. purpose
   d. separation

6. *hoc* (line 7) refers to
   a. the Ionian Sea
   b. the grandfather
   c. Arrius
   d. the uncle

7. In line 8, *eadem haec* refer to
   a. words
   b. family members
   c. ears
   d. ambushes

8. According to lines 5–8, Arrius' problem was due to
   a. the long time spent in Syria
   b. the condition of his ears
   c. the way his family talked
   d. the soft manner of his speech

9. From lines 9–12, we learn that Arrius
   a. was no longer afraid
   b. is sent a horrible message
   c. returned from Ionia
   d. had called Ionia Hionia

10. In line 12, *esse* is translated
    a. had been
    b. are
    c. were
    d. will be

Translation *Suggested time: 4 minutes*

Translate the passage below as literally as possible.

et tum mirifice sperabat se esse locutum,
cum quantum poterat dixerat hinsidias.

Long Essay *Suggested time: 30 minutes*

In a number of Catullus' poems, the poet speaks of elegance and inelegance. Discuss how Poem 84 could be considered one of these poems.

Support your assertions with references drawn from **throughout** the poem. All Latin words must be copied or their line numbers provided, AND they must be translated or paraphrased closely enough so that it is clear you understand the Latin. It is your responsibility to convince your reader that you are basing your conclusions on the Latin text and not merely on a general recollection of the passage. Direct your answer to the question; do not merely summarize the passage. Please write your essay on a separate piece of paper.

Scansion

Scan the following lines and name the meter.

hoc misso in Syriam requierant omnibus aures:

audibant eadem haec leniter et leviter,

CATULLUS 85

Odi et amo. quare id faciam, fortasse requiris?
nescio, sed fieri sentio et excrucior.

Short Answer Questions

Line 1   What is the mood and tense of *faciam?* _____

In what type of a clause is *faciam?* _____

Line 2   What grammatical form is *fieri?*_____

Multiple Choice Questions *Suggested time: 3 minutes*

1.   In line 1, there is an example of

  a. anaphora   b. an oxymoron

  c. hyperbaton   d. hendiadys

2.   In line 1, *id* refers to

  a. asking the question   b. what is being done

  c. tormenting her   d. why this is happening

3.   This poem contains more than one

  a. elision   b. hiatus

  c. diaeresis   d. synizesis

Translation *Suggested time: 4 minutes*

Translate the passage below as literally as possible.

Odi et amo. quare id faciam, fortasse requiris?
nescio, sed fieri sentio et excrucior.

_____

_____

_____

Short Essay *Suggested time: 20 minutes*

Catullus organized Poem 85 around verbs. Discuss the symmetrical structure of the eight verbs in this poem.

Support your assertions with references drawn from **throughout** the poem. All Latin words must be copied or their line numbers provided, AND they must be translated or paraphrased closely enough so that it is clear you understand the Latin. It is your responsibility to convince your reader that you are basing your conclusions on the Latin text and not merely on a general recollection of the passage. Direct your answer to the question; do not merely summarize the passage. Please write your essay on a separate piece of paper.

Scansion

Scan the following lines and name the meter.

Odi et amo. quare id faciam, fortasse requiris?

nescio, sed fieri sentio et excrucior.

CATULLUS 86

Quintia formosa est multis. mihi candida, longa,
 recta est: haec ego sic singula confiteor.
totum illud formosa nego: nam nulla venustas,
 nulla in tam magno est corpore mica salis.
5 Lesbia formosa est, quae cum pulcherrima tota est,
 tum omnibus una omnis surripuit Veneres.

Short Answer Questions

Line 1 What is the case and use of *multis?* _____

Line 2 What word does *singula* modify?_____

Line 3 What word does *totum* modify?_____

Line 4 What word does *nulla* modify? _____

Line 5 What is the case, use, and degree of *pulcherrima?* _____

    Translate *cum.* _____

Line 6 What is the case and use of *omnibus?* _____

    What word does *omnis* modify?_____

Multiple Choice Questions *Suggested time: 6 minutes*

1. In line 1, *mihi* refers to

  a. the poet   b. Quintia
  c. Lesbia   d. Venus

2. In line 2, *haec* refers to

  a. the singular beauty of Quintia b. several of Quintia's physical attributes
  c. Quintia's posture and personality d. Quintia herself

3. According to lines 3–4,

  a. Quintia has no real physical beauty b. the poet does not like Quintia
  c. the poet is in denial over Quintia d. Quintia's personality is lacking in some ways

4. Line 4 contains an example of

    a. chiasmus

    b. litotes

    c. pleonasm

    d. personification

5. The antecedent of *quae* (line 5) is

    a. *Quintia* (line 1)

    b. *venustas* (line 3)

    c. *Lesbia* (line 5)

    d. *formosa* (line 5)

Translation *Suggested time: 5 minutes*

Translate the passage below as literally as possible.

Lesbia formosa est, quae cum pulcherrima tota est,
tum omnibus una omnis surripuit Veneres.

_____

_____

_____

_____

Long Essay *Suggested time: 30 minutes*

How does the use of repetition enhance the meaning of the poem?

Support your assertions with references drawn from **throughout** the poem. All Latin words must be copied or their line numbers provided, AND they must be translated or paraphrased closely enough so that it is clear you understand the Latin. It is your responsibility to convince your reader that you are basing your conclusions on the Latin text and not merely on a general recollection of the passage. Direct your answer to the question; do not merely summarize the passage. Please write your essay on a separate piece of paper.

Scansion

Scan the following lines and name the meter.

Quintia formosa est multis. mihi candida, longa,

recta est: haec ego sic singula confiteor.

CATULLUS 87

Nulla potest mulier tantum se dicere amatam
vere, quantum a me Lesbia amata mea est.
nulla fides ullo fuit umquam foedere tanta,
quanta in amore tuo ex parte reperta mea est.

Short Answer Questions

Line 1   What word does *nulla* modify? _____

What is the case and use of *se?* _____

Line 2   What is the case and use of *me?* _____

Line 3   What word does *tanta* modify? _____

Line 4   What word does *mea* modify? _____

Multiple Choice Questions *Suggested time: 3 minutes*

1.   In line 1, *dicere* is

   a.   an infinitive in indirect statement

   b.   complementary to *potest*

   c.   an alternate second person singular present tense

   d.   a syncopated perfect active third person plural verb

2.   Line 2

   a.   is a hypermetric line

   b.   has more than one elision

   c.   features iambic shortening

   d.   does not contain a caesura

3.   To what type of an agreement does *foedere* in line 3 refer?

   a..   an agreement to be faithful to one another

   b.   an agreement to get married

   c.   an agreement to have faith in the gods

   d.   an agreement to share their wordly goods

Translation *Suggested time: 5 minutes*

Translate the passage below as literally as possible.

> **nulla fides ullo fuit umquam foedere tanta,**
> **quanta in amore tuo ex parte reperta mea est.**

_____

_____

_____

Short Essay *Suggested time: 20 minutes*

In Poem 87 Catullus expresses the deep love of a poet-lover for his mistress. Discuss how *fides* and *foedus* are linked, in Catullus' mind, to *amor*.

Support your assertions with references drawn from **throughout** the poem. All Latin words must be copied or their line numbers provided, AND they must be translated or paraphrased closely enough so that it is clear you understand the Latin. It is your responsibility to convince your reader that you are basing your conclusions on the Latin text and not merely on a general recollection of the passage. Direct your answer to the question; do not merely summarize the passage. Please write your essay on a separate piece of paper.

Scansion

Scan the following lines and name the meter.

nulla fides ullo fuit umquam foedere tanta,

quanta in amore tuo ex parte reperta mea est.

CATULLUS 96

Si quicquam mutis gratum acceptumve sepulcris
accidere a nostro, Calve, dolore potest,
quo desiderio veteres renovamus amores
atque olim missas flemus amicitias,
5   certe non tanto mors immatura dolori est
Quintiliae, quantum gaudet amore tuo.

Short Answer Questions

Line 1   What word does *acceptum* modify? _____

Line 2   What word does *nostro* modify? _____

Line 3   What is the case and use of *desiderio*? _____

Line 4   What is the tense, voice, and form of *missas*? _____

Line 5   What word does *tanto* modify? _____

            What is the case and use of *dolori*? _____

Line 6   Translate *amore tuo*. _____

Multiple Choice Questions *Suggested time: 6 minutes*

1. Line 1 contains an example of

    a. synecdoche   b. onomatopeia
    c. chiasmus   d. tmesis

2. According to lines 1–2, Calvus

    a. cannot talk because of his grief   b. is grateful that it was an easy death
    c. is grieving over the loss of someone d. accepted a silent tomb from somebody

3. In lines 3–4, the subject of *renovamus* and *flemus* refers to

    a. Calvus and the poet   b. Calvus and Quintilia
    c. Catullus and Quintilia   d. the poet and his girlfriend

4. From lines 5–6, we learn that

    a. Quintilia died at a young age   b. Quintilia was an immature girl
    c. Calvus' grief was untimely   d. Calvus was not sure Quintilia died

5. The subject of *gaudet* (line 6) refers to

    a. Quintilia
              b. Calvus' love

    c. Catullus
              d. Calvus

Translation *Suggested time: 5 minutes*

Translate the passage below as literally as possible.

quo desiderio veteres renovamus amores
atque olim missas flemus amicitias,

_____

_____

_____

Long Essay *Suggested time: 30 minutes*

Discuss the symmetrical structure of this six-line poem, which is integrated by both verbal similarities and contrasts, and explain how the structure enhances the poem's meaning.

Support your assertions with references drawn from **throughout** the poem. All Latin words must be copied or their line numbers provided, AND they must be translated or paraphrased closely enough so that it is clear you understand the Latin. It is your responsibility to convince your reader that you are basing your conclusions on the Latin text and not merely on a general recollection of the passage. Direct your answer to the question; do not merely summarize the passage. Please write your essay on a separate piece of paper.

Scansion

Scan the following lines and name the meter.

Si quicquam mutis gratum acceptumve sepulcris

accidere a nostro, Calve, dolore potest,

CATULLUS 101

Multas per gentes et multa per aequora vectus
    advenio has miseras, frater, ad inferias,
ut te postremo donarem munere mortis
    et mutam nequiquam alloquerer cinerem.
5   quandoquidem fortuna mihi tete abstulit ipsum,
    heu miser indigne frater adempte mihi,
nunc tamen interea haec, prisco quae more parentum
    tradita sunt tristi munere ad inferias,
accipe fraterno multum manantia fletu,
10   atque in perpetuum, frater, ave atque vale.

Short Answer Questions

Line 1   What does *vectus* modify?_____

Line 2   What is the case and use of *frater?*_____

Line 3   What is the mood and tense of *donarem?* _____

            What word does *postremo* modify? _____

Line 5   What is the case and use of *mihi?* _____

            What word does *ipsum* modify?_____

Line 6   What case is *adempte,* and what word does it modify?_____

Line 7   What word does *prisco* modify? _____

Line 8   What word does *tristi* modify?_____

Line 9   What case is *manantia,* and what word does it modify? _____

Multiple Choice Questions *Suggested time: 7 minutes*

1.   Line 1 contains an example of

    a. chiasmus   b. anaphora

    c. hysteron proteron   d. hyperbole

2.   In line 4, *alloquerer* is in a(n)

    a. result clause   b. indirect question

    c. purpose clause   d. indirect command

3. In line 5, *mihi* refers to
   a. the subject of *advenio* (line 2)
   b. *cinerem* (line 4)
   c. the word *ipsum* modifies (line 5)
   d. *frater* (line 6)

4. Which of the following is **not** mentioned in lines 1–6?
   a. that Catullus traveled quite far to visit his brother's grave
   b. that Catullus feels responsible for his brother's death
   c. that Catullus is bringing a gift to his brother's grave
   d. that Catullus feels his brother's death was undeserved

5. The antecedent of *quae* in line 7 is
   a. *fortuna* (line 5)
   b. *haec* (line 7)
   c. *munere* (line 8)
   d. *inferias* (line 8)

6. By the end of Poem 101, we know that Catullus
   a. acts differently from the way his ancestors did
   b. is too sad to put an offering at his brother's gravesite
   c. is crying quite a bit as he says good-bye to his brother
   d. feels his brother deserves what has happened

Translation *Suggested time: 10 minutes*

Translate the passage below as literally as possible.

> nunc tamen interea haec, prisco quae more parentum
> tradita sunt tristi munere ad inferias,
> accipe fraterno multum manantia fletu,
> atque in perpetuum, frater, ave atque vale.

_____

_____

_____

_____

_____

Long Essay *Suggested time: 30 minutes*

A feeling of sadness pervades Poem 101. Discuss the ways in which Catullus conveys his feelings of sadness in this poem.

Support your assertions with references drawn from **throughout** the poem. All Latin words must be copied or their line numbers provided, AND they must be translated or paraphrased closely enough so that it is clear you understand the Latin. It is your responsibility to convince your reader that you are basing your conclusions on the Latin text and not merely on a general recollection of the passage. Direct your answer to the question; do not merely summarize the passage. Please write your essay on a separate piece of paper.

Scansion

Scan the following lines and name the meter.

Multas per gentes et multa per aequora vectus

advenio has miseras, frater, ad inferias,

CATULLUS 109

Iucundum, mea vita, mihi proponis amorem
    hunc nostrum inter nos perpetuumque fore.
di magni, facite ut vere promittere possit,
    atque id sincere dicat et ex animo,
5   ut liceat nobis tota perducere vita
    aeternum hoc sanctae foedus amicitiae.

Short Answer Questions

Line 1   What is the case and use of *vita?* _____

Line 2   What is the alternate form of *fore?* _____

Line 3   What is the mood and tense of *possit?* _____

Line 4   What is the case and use of *animo?* _____

Line 5   What is the case and use of *nobis?* _____

Line 6   What does *hoc* modify? _____

Multiple Choice Questions *Suggested time: 7 minutes*

1.   In lines 1–2, there is an example of
    a. hypermetry
    c. synizesis
    b. elision
    d. enjambment

2.   From lines 1–2, we learn that
    a. a love relationship is being discussed
    c. love will make life go on forever
    b. Catullus is proposing to his love
    d. love will not make life pleasant

3.   The subject of *possit* (line 3) refers to
    a. Catullus
    c. love
    b. a great god
    d. Catullus' lover

4.   In line 4, *dicat* is in a(n)
    a. purpose clause
    c. noun clause of fact
    b. indirect command
    d. indirect question

5. *id* (line 4) refers to

   a. her promise

   b. her sincerity

   c. her truthfulness

   d. her life

6. In line 5, *liceat* is in a(n)

   a. result clause

   b. noun clause of fact

   c. indirect command

   d. fear clause

7. Line 6 contains an example of

   a. hendiadys

   b. metonymy

   c. irony

   d. synchysis

Translation *Suggested time: 4 minutes*

Translate the passage below as literally as possible.

di magni, facite ut vere promittere possit,
atque id sincere dicat et ex animo,

_____

_____

_____

_____

Long Essay *Suggested time: 30 minutes*

Poem 109 presents a contrast. Discuss the ways in which Catullus makes this contrast clear.

Support your assertions with references drawn from **throughout** the poem. All Latin words must be copied or their line numbers provided, AND they must be translated or paraphrased closely enough so that it is clear you understand the Latin. It is your responsibility to convince your reader that you are basing your conclusions on the Latin text and not merely on a general recollection of the passage. Direct your answer to the question; do not merely summarize the passage. Please write your essay on a separate piece of paper.

Scansion

Scan the following lines and name the meter.

ut liceat nobis tota perducere vita

aeternum hoc sanctae foedus amicitiae.

CATULLUS 116

Saepe tibi studioso animo venante requirens
    carmina uti possem mittere Battiadae,
qui te lenirem nobis, neu conarere
    tela infesta <meum> mittere in usque caput,
5   hunc video mihi nunc frustra sumptum esse laborem,
    Gelli, nec nostras hic valuisse preces.
contra nos tela ista tua evitabimus acta,
    at fixus nostris tu dabis supplicium.

Short Answer Questions

Line 1   What is the case and use of *venante?* _____

Line 2   What is the mood and tense of *possem?* _____

Line 3   What is the person, number, and tense of *conarere?* _____

Line 4   To what verb is *mittere* a complementary infinitive? _____

Line 5   What word does *hunc* modify? _____

            What is the case and use of *mihi?* _____

Line 6   What is the case and use of *Gelli?* _____

            What is the tense and voice of *valuisse?* _____

Line 7   What word does *acta* modify? _____

Multiple Choice Questions *Suggested time: 7 minutes*

1.   In line 1, *tibi* refers to

    a. the poet   b. Gellius

    c. Catullus   d. Callimachus

2.   In line 2, *Battiadae* refers to

    a. the poet   b. Gellius

    c. Callimachus   d. a hunter

3. Which of these is **not** a correct translation of *qui* in line 3?

   a. whereby   b. so that

   c. by which   d. who

4. Line 3 is a

   a. spondaic line   b. golden line

   c. pentameter line   d. hypermetric line

5. According to lines 1–4,

   a. Callimachus is shooting hostile weapons at Catullus   b. Catullus is looking for poems to send to Gellius

   c. Battiades is hunting for Catullus' head   d. Gellius is trying to reconcile with Catullus

6. In line 5, *sumptum esse* is a(n)

   a. complementary infinitive   b. subjective infinitive

   c. infinitive in an indirect statement   d. infinitive with an impersonal verb

7. From lines 5–8, it is evident that

   a. there is still a disagreement   b. the problem has been solved by working it out

   c. prayers have been made over the settlement   d. they avoided throwing any weapons

Translation *Suggested time: 5 minutes*

Translate the passage below as literally as possible.

> **hunc video mihi nunc frustra sumptum esse laborem,**
> **Gelli, nec nostras hic valuisse preces.**

_____

_____

_____

_____

Short Essay *Suggested time: 20 minutes*

Discuss the imagery that Catullus uses to convey the meaning of Poem 116.

Support your assertions with references drawn from **throughout** the poem. All Latin words must be copied or their line numbers provided, AND they must be translated or paraphrased closely enough so that it is clear you understand the Latin. It is your responsibility to convince your reader that you are basing your conclusions on the Latin text and not merely on a general recollection of the passage. Direct your answer to the question; do not merely summarize the passage. Please write your essay on a separate piece of paper.

Scansion

Scan the following lines and name the meter.

Saepe tibi studioso animo venante requirens

carmina uti possem mittere Battiadae,

REVIEW FOUR

Poems 69, 70, 72, 76, 77, 84, 85, 86, 87, 96, 101, 109, 116

Match the person to Catullus' description.

1. ____ Arrius
2. ____ Gellius
3. ____ Lesbia
4. ____ Rufus
5. ____ Quintilia

A. valle sub alarum trux habitare caper.

B. Nulla potest mulier tantum se dicere amatam/ vere, . . .

C. certe non tanto mors immatura dolori est . . .

D. at fixus nostris tu dabis supplicium.

E. et tum mirifice sperabat se esse locutum,

Below are quotations from Catullus' poems. Explain to whom or what the words in bold refer.

1. Dicebas quondam solum **te** nosse Catullum, _____

2. eripite hanc pestem perniciemque **mihi**, _____

3. et mutam nequiquam alloquerer **cinerem**. _____

4. Iucundum, mea **vita**, mihi proponis amorem _____

5. qui **te** lenirem nobis, _____

6. laedit **te** quaedam mala fabula, _____

7. ipse valere opto et taetrum hunc deponere **morbum**. _____

8. heu heu nostrae crudele **venenum**/ vitae, _____

9. Nulli **se** dicit **mulier** mea nubere malle _____

10. quandoquidem fortuna **mihi** tete abstulit ipsum, _____

Many types of subjunctive uses are found in Catullus' poetry. Identify the type of subjunctive found in each of the following lines and then translate the entire line.

1. non si se Iuppiter ipse petat

    _____

    _____

2. quare id faciam, fortasse requiris

    _____

    _____

3. hoc facias, sive id non potes sive pote

    _____

    _____

4. facite ut . . . id sincere dicat et ex animo

    _____

    _____

5. ut te postremo donarem munere mortis

    _____

    _____

Long Essay *Suggested time: 30 minutes*

Siqua recordanti benefacta priora voluptas
    est homini, cum se cogitat esse pium,
nec sanctam violasse fidem, nec foedere nullo
    divum ad fallendos numine abusum homines,
5   multa parata manent in longa aetate, Catulle,
    ex hoc ingrato gaudia amore tibi.
nam quaecumque homines bene cuiquam aut dicere possunt
    aut facere, haec a te dictaque factaque sunt.
omnia quae ingratae perierunt credita menti.
10   quare iam te cur amplius excrucies?
quin tu animo offirmas atque istinc teque reducis,
    et dis invitis desinis esse miser?
difficile est longum subito deponere amorem,
    difficile est, verum hoc qua lubet efficias:
15   una salus haec est, hoc est tibi pervincendum,
    hoc facias, sive id non pote sive pote.
o di, si vestrum est misereri, aut si quibus umquam
    extremam iam ipsa in morte tulistis opem,
me miserum aspicite et, si vitam puriter egi,
20   eripite hanc pestem perniciemque mihi,
quae mihi subrepens imos ut torpor in artus
    expulit ex omni pectore laetitias.
non iam illud quaero, contra me ut diligat illa,
    aut, quod non potis est, esse pudica velit:
25   ipse valere opto et taetrum hunc deponere morbum.
    o di, reddite mi hoc pro pietate mea.

Catullus 76

Rufe mihi frustra ac nequiquam credite amice
    (frustra? immo magno cum pretio atque malo),
sicine subrepsti mi, atque intestina perurens
    ei misero eripuisti omnia nostra bona?
5   eripuisti, heu heu nostrae crudele venenum
    vitae, heu heu nostrae pestis amicitiae.

Catullus 77

The language found in lines 19–26 of Poem 76 is echoed in lines 1–6 of Poem 77. Discuss how this repetition of language is significant for the interpretation of the second of the two poems.

Scansion

Scan the following lines and name the meter.

una salus haec est, hoc est tibi pervincendum,

hoc facias, sive id non pote sive pote.

o di, si vestrum est misereri, aut si quibus umquam

extremam iam ipsa in morte tulistis opem,

VOCABULARY*

In general, only long vowels in metrically indeterminate positions are marked. For example, the length of the *a* in "annus" need not be marked as long or short because the syllable in which it is contained must be long, regardless of the length of the vowel, because the vowel is followed by two consonants, "nn," (not a combination like *tr* which can create indeterminacy), while the *a* in "beātus" must be marked long because it occurs in a position where metrical rules cannot determine the length of the syllable in which it occurs. Genitive singular of second declension nouns whose nominative singular ends in "-ius" or "-ium" is given as ī (not iī) since that was the form in use when Catullus wrote. These words have the whole word written in the genitive rather than just ī, e.g., "Cornelius, Cornelī" vs. "scriptum, -ī." These genitives accent the penult, even when short. The same holds for the accent in the vocative of second declension proper names ending in "-ius," e.g., "Cornélī."

A

ā, *interj.*, ah; *interjection expressing a variety of feelings*

ā/ab, *prep. with abl.*, from, by

abeō, abīre, abiī, abitum, go away, depart, get off, be allowed to pass

abhorreō, abhorrēre, abhorruī, shrink back from, be averse to, be different from

absūmō, absūmere, absumpsī, absumptum, spend, consume, wear out, exhaust, destroy, remove by death

abūtor, abūtī, abūsum, use up, use, abuse, take advantage of

ac, *conj.*, and

acceptus, -a, -um, *adj.*, welcome, pleasing

accidō, accidere, accidī, fall down, happen, come to pass, arise

accipiō, accipere, accēpī, acceptum, receive, take, hear, understand

ācer, ācris, ācre, *adj.*, sharp, fierce, eager, dangerous

acerbus, -a, -um, bitter, harsh, untimely (esp. of death)

aciēs, aciēī, *f.*, sharp edge, eye, battle line

Acmē, Acmēs, *f.*, Acme, a woman's name.

acquiescō, acquiescere, acquiē(v)ī, rest, relax, subside, find relief

ad, *prep. with acc.*, to, towards, near

adeō, adīre, ad(i)ī, aditum, go to, approach

adferō, adferre, attulī, allātum, bring, add

adimō, adimere, adēmī, ademptum, take away

admīror, admīrārī, admīrātus sum, be surprised at, wonder at, admire

adveniō, advenīre, advēnī, adventum, come to, reach

adventō, adventāre, adventāvī, adventātum, approach, draw near

adventus, -ūs, *m.*, arrival, approach

adversus, -a, -um, *adj.*, turned toward, opposite, hostile

advocō, advocāre, advocāvī, advocātum, call upon, summon, invoke the aid of the gods, employ as legal counsel

Aegeus, Aegeī, *m.*, Aegeus, legendary king of Athens, father of Theseus

aequē, *adv.*, equally

* The glossary of the present work appeared in a slightly different version in *Writing Passion: A Catullus Reader*, by Ronnie Ancona Bolchazy-Carducci Publishers (2004): 221–263. ©2004 by Bolchazy-Carducci Publishers.

• 217 •

aequinoctiālis, aequinoctiāle, *adj.*, connected with the equinox, equinoctial

aequō, aequāre, aequāvī, aequātum, make level, even, smooth

aequor, aequoris, *n.*, a flat level surface, the flat surface of the sea, sea *(often used in pl.)*

āereus (āerius), -a, -um, *adj.*, reaching high into the air, lofty, tall

aes, aeris, *n.*, copper, bronze, money

aestimātiō, aestimātiōnis, *f.*, valuation, estimation, monetary worth

aestimō, aestimāre, aestimāvī, aestimātum, value, assess at

aestuōsus, -a, -um, *adj.*, very hot, agitated

aestus, -ūs, *m.*, heat, passion, tide

aetās, aetātis, *f.*, time, age

aeternus, -a, -um, *adj.*, eternal, everlasting

aevum, -ī, *n.*, time, age, course of history

afferō, afferre, attulī, allātum, bring, deliver

ager, agrī, *m.*, field, territory

agnoscō, agnoscere, agnōvī, agnōtum, recognize, identify

agō, agere, ēgī, actum, do, drive, propel

āiō, *defective verb*, say yes, say

āla, -ae, *f.*, wing, armpit

āles, ālitis, *m., f.*, large bird; omen

Alfenus, -a, -um, *adj.*, name of a Roman **gens**

alga, -ae, *f.*, seaweed

aliquis, aliqua, aliquid, *pron.*, someone, anyone, something, anything

alius, alia, aliud, *adj.*, other, another

alloquor, alloquī, allocūtus sum, speak to, address, invoke, comfort

allūdō, allūdere, allūsī, allūsum, play against, play with

alluō, alluere, alluī, flow past, wash, wet

alō, alere, aluī, altum, nourish

Alpēs, Alpium, *f. pl.*, the Alps, high mountains bordering Italy on the north

alter, altera, alterum, *adj.*, another, one of two, the one, the other

altus, -a, -um, *adj.*, high, deep, tall

amābilis, -e, *adj.*, able or worthy to be loved, delightful

amans, amantis, *m., f.*, lover

amāritiēs, amāritiēī, *f.*, bitterness

Amastris, Amastridis, *f.*, town in Paphlagonia, a country in Asia Minor between Bithynia and Pontus

Amathūs, Amathuntis, *f.*, town in Cyprus connected with worship of Venus

ambō, ambae, ambō, *pl. adj. and pron.*, both, two of a pair

āmens, āmentis, *adj.*, demented, insane, frantic

amīca, -ae, *f.*, female friend, girlfriend

amīcitia, -ae, *f.*, friendship, accord

amictus, -ūs, *m.*, cloak, clothing

amīculus, -ī, *m.*, dear friend, dear lover

amīcus, -ī, *m.*, friend, lover

āmittō, āmittere, āmīsī, āmissum, send away, release, lose

amō, amāre, amāvī, amātum, love, make love

amor, amōris, *m.*, love, sexual passion, object of one's love *(usually in pl.)*, love affair, act of sex; love PERSONIFIED as the god of love

amplius, *adv.*, more, further

an, *particle.*, whether, or

Ancōna, -ae, *f.*, Ancona, seaport on the Adriatic coast of Italy in Picenum settled by Greeks

Androgeōnēus, -a, -um, *adj.*, of Androgeos, son of Minos and Pasiphae.

anguīnus, -a, -um, *adj.*, of snakes, consisting of snakes

angustus, -a, -um, *adj.*, narrow, limited, difficult (of circumstances)

anima, -ae, *f.*, breath, life, darling

animus, -ī, *m.*, mind, inclination, desire, enthusiasm, feelings

annālis, annālis, *m.* (short for **annālis liber**), book of annals, chronicles; *pl.*, chronicle or similar history written in several books, records, history

annuō, annuere, annuī, annūtum, make signs, nod, nod assent, approve of

annus, -ī, *m.*, year

ante, *adv.*, before, previously, in front; *prep. with acc.*, before, in front of

anteā, *adv.*, previously

antenna, -ae, *f.*, sailyard, sail

Antius, Antī, *m.*, possibly the Gaius Antius who was responsible for a sumptuary law aimed at electoral corruption

anxius, -a, -um, *adj.*, disturbed, distressing

apertus, -a, -um, *adj.*, open, exposed to the elements

apiscor, apiscī, aptus sum, grasp, get

appāreō, appārēre, appāruī, appāritum, appear

appetō, appetere, appetīvī/appetiī, appetītum, seek, desire, attack

approbātiō, approbātiōnis, *f.*, approbation, giving of one's approval

apud, *prep. with acc.*, at, near, at the house of, with (a person)

aqua, -ae, *f.*, water, body of water

Aquīnus, -a, -um, *adj.*, name of a Roman **gens**

āra, -ae, *f.*, altar, refuge

Arabēs, Arabum, *m. pl.*, Arabs

arānea, -ae, *f.*, spider's web, cobweb, spider

arātrum, -ī, *n.*, plough

ardeō, ardēre, arsī, be on fire, burn, be in love

ardor, ardōris, *m.*, burning, fierce heat, passion

Ariadna, -ae, *f.*, Ariadne, daughter of King Minos of Crete and his wife, Pasiphae.

āridus, -a, -um, *adj.*, dry, lacking embellishment

Arrius, Arrī, *m.*, Arrius; most likely Quintus Arrius, self-made orator and follower of the triumvir, Marcus Licinius Crassus

ars, artis, *f.*, art, technical skill, craft, method

artus, artūs, *m.*, joint, limb, arm or leg, member or part of body

arx, arcis, *f.*, citadel, height

as, assis, *m.*, coin of small value, penny

Asia, -ae, *f.*, Asia, Asia Minor, the East, Roman province of Asia

Asinius, -a, -um, *adj.*, the name of a Roman **gens**

aspiciō, aspicere, aspexī, aspectum, catch sight of, look at, gaze upon, see, behold

assiduē, *adv.*, continually, constantly

assiduus, -a, -um, *adj.*, persistent, constant

at, *conj.*, but, however, yet

Athēnae, -ārum, *f. pl.*, Athens

atque, *conj.*, and; after comparatives, than

attingō, attingere, attigī, attactum, touch, reach, take up (a task)

attribuō, attribuere, attribuī, attribūtum, assign, count as belonging to, ascribe as an attribute

audax, audācis, *adj.*, daring, bold, rash

audeō, audēre, ausus sum, dare, wish

audiō, audīre, audīvī, audītum, hear, heed

auferō, auferre, abstulī, ablātum, take away, carry off, kill

augeō, augēre, auxī, auctum, increase, furnish

aura, -ae, *f.*, breeze; **aureīs** (archaic) = **aurīs**

Aurēlius, Aurēlī, *m.*, Aurelius; not identified outside of Catullus' poems

auris, auris, *f.*, ear

aurum -ī, *n.*, gold

auspicātus, -a, -um, *adj.*, approved by augury, auspicious, fortunate, lucky

auspicium, auspicī, *n.*, auspices, observing of omens from birds, omen, fortune, luck

aut, *conj.*, or; **aut . . . aut**, either . . . or

autem, *particle*, but, moreover

autumō, autumāre, autumāvī, autumātum, allege, affirm, say, call, think

auxilium, auxilī, *n.*, help, aid

avē (formal expression of greeting), hail

āvehō, āvehere, āvehī, āvectum, carry off, depart

aveō, avēre, be eager, desire, long

avia, -ae, *f.*, grandmother

avunculus, -ī, *m.*, maternal uncle; a mother's sister's husband

avus, -ī, *m.*, grandfather, ancestor

B

bacchor, bacchārī, bacchātus sum, celebrate the festival of Bacchus, rave, rage

bāsiātiō, bāsiātiōnis, *f.*, a kissing or kiss

bāsiō, bāsiāre, bāsiāvī, bāsiātum, kiss

bāsium, bāsī, *n.*, kiss

Battiadēs, -ae, *m.*, an inhabitant of Cyrene, town of northwest Libya, whose legendary founder was Battus; specifically Callimachus

Battus, -ī, *m.*, Battus, legendary founder of Cyrene

beātus, -a, -um, *adj.*, happy, fortunate

bellē, *adv.*, nicely, well

bellus, -a, -um, *adj.*, charming, handsome, pretty, fine

bene, *adv.*, well; *with adj. or adv.*, quite

benefactum, -ī, *n.*, good deed, benefit, service

bestia, -ae, *f.*, beast, animal, creature

Bīthūnius (Bīthȳnius), -a, -um, *adj.*, Bithynian

Bīthȳnia, -ae, Bithynia; Roman province on the northwest coast of Asia Minor; Catullus served there on the staff of Gaius Memmius, governor in 57–56 BCE.

blandus, -a, -um, *adj.,* charming, persuasive, seductive

bonus, -a, -um, *adj.,* good

brāchium, brāchī, *n.,* arm

brevis, -e, *adj.,* short, brief

Britannī, Britannōrum, *m. pl.,* inhabitants of Britain, Britons

Britannia, -ae, *f.,* Britain

buxifer, buxifera, buxiferum, *adj.,* producing box trees

C

c(h)arta, -ae, *f.,* sheet of papyrus, writings, roll (with one sheet standing for plural)

cachinnus, -ī, *m.,* laugh

cacō, cacāre, cacāvī, cacātum, defecate, emit as excrement

cacūmen, cacūminis, *n.,* peak, top

cadō, cadere, cecidī, cāsum, fall, die, set (of heavenly bodies)

Caecilius, Caecilī, *m.,* Caecilius; otherwise unknown

caecus, -a, -um, *adj.,* blind, dark, hidden

caedēs, caedis, *f.,* killing, slaughter

caelebs, caelibis, *adj.,* unmarried

caeles, caelitis, *adj.,* celestial; *as noun, usually plural,* a god

caelestis, -e, *adj.,* of the sky, celestial, divine

caelicola, -ae, *m.,* or *f.,* inhabitant of heaven, a god or goddess

caelum, -ī, *n.,* sky, heavens, weather, world

caeruleus, -a, -um, *adj.,* blue

Caesar, Caesaris, *m.,* Julius Caesar, the famous Roman general and politician, 100–44 BCE; friend of Catullus' family; attacked by Catullus in several poems.

Caesius, -a, -um, *adj.,* name of a Roman **gens**

caesius, -a, -um, *adj.,* gray or gray-blue, having gray or gray-blue eyes

cālīgō, cālīginis, *f.,* darkness, obscurity of a mist or fog

Calvus, -ī *m.,* Gaius Licinius Calvus, 82–47 BCE, intimate friend of Catullus; poet, orator

campus, -ī, *m.,* plain, level surface; field; often refers specifically to the Campus Martius in Rome

candidus, -a, -um, *adj.,* bright, radiant, white

canitiēs, canitiēī, *f.,* white or grey coloring, grey or white hair

canō, canere, cecinī, cantum, sing, sing about, recite, prophesy, foretell

caper, caprī, *m.,* male goat; by METONYMY, goat-like smell

capillus, -ī, *m.,* hair

capiō, capere, cēpī, captum, take, capture, get

caprimulgus, -ī, *m.,* country bumpkin (from **capra, -ae,** *f.,* she-goat, and **mulgeō,** milk)

capsula, -ae, *f.,* small container for books

caput, capitis, *n.,* head, top, source, person, person's life

carbasus, -ī, *f.,* sail, canvas, awning

carīna, -ae, *f.,* bottom of a ship, ship, boat

carmen, carminis, *n.,* solemn or ritual utterance, song, poem, lyric poetry

carpō, carpere, carpsī, carptum, pluck, seize, wear away, consume

cārus, -a, -um, *adj.,* dear, beloved

Carybdis, Carybdis, *f.,* whirlpool, seen as female monster, on Sicilian side of strait between Sicily and Italy

Castor, Castoris, *m.,* Castor, son of Tyndareus (or Zeus) and Leda, and brother of Pollux; Castor and Pollux, also called the Dioscuri, are a help at sea

castus, -a, -um, *adj.,* pure, virgin, sexually faithful

cāsus, -ūs, *m.,* fall, event, misfortune, chance

Catullus, -ī, *m.,* Gaius Valerius Catullus, the poet

caveō, cavēre, cāvī, cautum, beware, refrain from, watch out for

Cecropia, -ae, *f.,* Athens; from Cecrops, legendary king of Athens

cēdō, cēdere, cessī, cessum, go, yield, withdraw

celer, celeris, celere, *adj.,* swift, quick

cēlō, cēlāre, cēlāvī, cēlātum, conceal, hide

cēna, -ae, *f.,* dinner

cēnō, cēnāre, cēnāvī, cēnātum, dine, have dinner

centum, *indecl. adj.,* a hundred

cernō, cernere, crēvī, crētum, distinguish, see, perceive, decide

certē, *adv.,* certainly

ceu, *particle,* as, like

cibus, -ī, *m.,* food, meal, sustenance

cieō, ciēre, cīvī, citum, stir up, rouse, produce

cinaedus, -a, -um, *adj.,* resembling or typical of a **cinaedus** or gender transgressive man, i.e., one who plays a "passive" sexual role; can be used of a female, shameless, sluttish

cingō, cingere, cinxī, cinctum, surround, encircle

cinis, cineris, *m., f.,* ashes

Cinna, -ae, *m.,* Gaius Helvius Cinna, poet contemporary with Catullus who likely served with him in Bithynia; killed by a mob at Caesar's funeral when mistaken for the anti-Caesarian, Lucius Cornelius Cinna

circumsiliō, circumsilīre, leap or jump around

clārisonus, -a, -um, *adj.,* loud or clear sounding

clārus, -a, -um, *adj.,* clear, bright, famous

classis, classis, *f.,* fleet, political class

clēmentia, -ae, *f.,* clemency, disposition to pardon, mildness

cliens, clientis, *m.,* client; one who attaches himself to a person of greater influence or political power (**patrōnus**) for protection

Cnidus, -ī, *f.,* Cnidus, town in southwest Asia Minor with three temples to Venus

Cnōsius (Gnōsius), -a, -um, related to city of Cnossos on Crete or, to Crete

coetus, coetūs, *m.,* meeting, crowd, band, company, gang

cōgitātiō, cōgitātiōnis, *f.,* thought, deliberation

cōgitō, cōgitāre, cōgitāvī, cōgitātum, think, consider, imagine, recollect

cognitus, -a, -um, *adj.,* known, noted

cognoscō, cognoscere, cognōvī, cognitum, get to know, have experience of

cōgō, cōgere, coēgī, coactum, drive together, force

cohors, cohortis, *f.,* cohort, staff of a governor or other official

colligō, colligere, collēgī, collectum, to gather or bring together, collect

collis, collis, *m.,* hill

collocō, collocāre, collocāvī, collocātum, put, place

collum, -ī, *n.,* neck

colō, colere, coluī, cultum, cultivate, cherish

color, colōris, *m.,* color

colōrō, colōrāre, colōrāvī, colōrātum, give color to, dye, make darker in color

coma, -ae, *f.,* hair, fleece, foliage

comātus, -a, -um, *adj.,* having long hair, leafy

comes, comitis, *m., f.,* one who goes with or accompanies another, companion, friend, comrade

commemorō, commemorāre, commemorāvī, commemorātum, recall, relate, tell

commodō, commodāre, commodāvī, commodātum, lend, provide

commodum, -ī, *n.,* advantage, benefit, gift, interest

comparō, comparāre, comparāvī, comparātum, compare, treat as equal to another

complector, complectī, complexus sum, embrace, hug

complexus, -ūs, *m.,* embrace

comprecor, comprecārī, comprecātus sum, pray to, invoke, supplicate

concēdō, concēdere, concessī, concessum, go away, concede, grant, allow

concinō, concinere, concinuī, sing together, celebrate in song

concipiō, concipere, concēpī, conceptum, take in, conceive, produce

concrēdō, concrēdere, concrēdidī, concrēditum, entrust for safekeeping

concutiō, concutere, concussī, concussum, shake, upset, stir up

condō, condere, condidī, conditum, found, establish, store up

conficio, conficere, confēcī, confectum, exhaust, complete

confiteor, confitērī, confessus sum, admit

cōniger, cōnigera, cōnigerum, coniferous, cone-bearing

coniunx, coniugis, *m., f.,* spouse, wife, husband

cōnor, cōnārī, cōnātus sum, attempt, try, make an effort

conqueror, conquerī, conquestus sum, complain, lament

consanguinea, -ae, *f.,* sister

conscendō, conscendere, conscendī, conscensum, climb, go up to

conscius, -a, -um, *adj.,* sharing knowledge, conscious, guilty

conscrībō, conscrībere, conscripsī, conscriptum, enroll, write on, compose

conserō, conserere, consēvī, consitum, sow, plant; **consitus** (of persons) beset

consilium, consilī, *n.,* deliberation, decision, purpose

consōlor, consōlārī, consōlātus sum, comfort, console

conspiciō, conspicere, conspexī, conspectum, catch sight of

constans, constantis, *adj.*, unchanging, constant

consternō, consternere, constrāvī, constrātum, spread, cover

contegō, contegere, contexī, contectum, clothe, cover, hide

contemnō, contemnere, contempsī, contemptum, look down on, despise, insult

contendō, contendere, contendī, contentum, stretch, hasten, compete, contend

continuō, *adv.*, immediately, continuously

contorqueō, contorquēre, contorsī, contortum, twist, whirl, turn about

contrā, *adv.*, in return; *prep. with acc.*, against

contremescō, contremescere, contremuī, tremble, be afraid of

conturbō, conturbāre, conturbāvī, conturbātum, mix up, go bankrupt

cōnūbium, cōnūbī, *n.*, marriage

conveniō, convenīre, convēnī, conventum, meet, agree, be suitable; *impers.*, it is agreed

convīva, -ae, *m., f.*, table companion, guest

cōpia, -ae, *f.*, large quantity, abundance, supply

cor, cordis, *n.*, heart

Cornelius, Cornelī, *m.*, Cornelius Nepos, c. 110–24 BCE, Latin biographer, historian, writer of light verse

cornū, -ūs, *n.*, horn, anything horn-shaped

corpus, corporis, *n.*, body

cortex, corticis, *m.*, bark, rind, cork

crēdō, crēdere, crēdidī, crēditum, trust, believe, entrust

creō, creāre, creāvī, creātum, create, bring into being

Crēta, -ae, *f.*, island of Crete

crūdēlis, -e, *adj.*, cruel, savage, painful

cubīle, cubīlis, *n.*, bed, couch

cubō, cubāre, cubuī, cubitum, lie down or be lying down, recline, be in bed or on one's couch, be confined to bed by illness, recline at table

culpa, -ae, *f.*, blame, fault, wrongdoing

cum, *prep. with abl.*, with; *conj.*, when, since, although

cunctus, -a, -um, *adj.*, the whole of, all

cupīdō, cupīdinis, *f., m.*, passionate desire, carnal desire, greed, PERSONIFICATION of carnal desire; *m.*, often regarded as a god, the son of Venus, Cupid

cupidus, -a, -um, *adj.*, having strong desire, longing, eager

cupiō, cupere, cupīvī, cupītum, wish, desire, long for

cūr, *adv.*, why, on account of which

cūra, -ae, *f.*, care, concern, worry, a person or thing constituting an object of care

cūriōsus, -a, -um, *adj.*, careful, diligent, curious, interfering

cūrō, cūrāre, cūrāvī, cūrātum, care about, take care of, attend to

currō, currere, cucurrī, cursum, run

curvus, -a, -um, *adj.*, bent, curved, winding

Cyclas, Cycladis/Cyclados, *f.*, one of the Cyclades, the islands in the Aegean Sea surrounding Delos

Cȳrēnae, -ārum, *f. pl.*, Cyrene, town of northwest Libya, district which surrounded the town and together with Crete became the province of Cyrene ; birthplace of Callimachus and Berenice II

Cytōrius, -a, -um, *adj.*, of Mount Cytorus in Paphlagonia

Cytōrus, -ī, *m.*, a mountain of Paphlagonia, country in Asia Minor between Bithynia and Pontus

D

daps, dapis, *f.*, feast, banquet

Daulias, Dauliados, *f. adj.*, of Daulis, a town in Phocis, region in central Greece where Delphi is located

dē, *prep. with abl.*, about, concerning, down from, from

dea, -ae, *f.*, goddess

decem, *indecl. adj.*, ten

decet, decēre, decuit, *impers.*, be right or fitting for, become

dēclīnō, dēclīnāre, dēclīnāvī, dēclīnātum, turn away

dēcoctor, dēcoctōris, *m.*, bankrupt person

dēcursus, -ūs, *m.*, descent, fall, downward flow

decus, decoris, *n.*, that which adorns or beautifies, honor, glory

dēdicō, dēdicāre, dēdicāvī, dēdicātum, dedicate

defendō, defendere, defendī, defensum, avert, defend, protect

dēferō, dēferre, dētulī, dēlātum, carry, convey, confer, grant

dēfessus, -a, -um, *adj.*, tired out, exhausted

dein/deinde, *adv.*, afterwards, then, next

dēlābor, dēlābī, dēlapsus sum, drop, slip down

dēlicātus, -a, -um, *adj.*, interested in pleasure, self-indulgent, elegant, effeminate

dēlicia, -ae, *f.*, *(usually in pl.)* pleasure, delight, sweetheart, pet, pet animal, toys, erotic verse

dēmānō, dēmānāre, dēmānāvī, run down

dēnique, *adv.*, finally

densus, -a, -um, *adj.*, thick, dense

dēperditus, -a, -um, *adj.*, abandoned, utterly lost

dēpereō, deperīre, deperiī, die, perish, be desperately in love with

dēpōnō, dēpōnere, dēposuī, dēpositum, put down, lay down, abandon

dēprecor, dēprecārī, dēprecātus sum, try to avert by prayer, beg

dēserō, dēserere, dēseruī, dēsertum, leave, abandon

dēsertus, -a, -um, *adj.*, deserted, uninhabited, left alone

dēsīderium, dēsīderī, *n.*, desire, longing, object of desire, darling

dēsīderō, dēsīderāre, dēsīderāvī, dēsīderātum, desire, want, long for

dēsinō, dēsinere, dēsiī, dēsitum, stop, cease

despuō, despuere, spit down on the ground, spurn, reject

dēstinātus, -a, -um, *adj.*, stubborn, obstinate

dēsum, dēesse, dēfuī, be missing, fail *(with dat. of person)*

deus, -ī, *m.*, god

dēvinciō, dēvincīre, dēvinxī, dēvinctum, bind

dēvorō, dēvorāre, dēvorāvī, dēvorātum, swallow, engulf, absorb

dēvōtus, -a, -um, *adj.*, accursed, devoted

dexter, dext(e)ra, dext(e)rum, *adj.*, right, skillful, coming from the right

dextrā, *adv.*, on the right

dextra, -ae, *f.*, right hand, pledge

Dīa, -ae, *f.*, island in the Aegean Sea, may refer to Naxos

dicax, dicācis, *adj.*, having a ready tongue, verbally witty

dicō, dicāre, dicāvī, dicātum, show, indicate

dīcō, dīcere, dixī, dictum, say, tell, call, sing, recite

dictum, -ī, *n.*, that which is said, words

diēs, diēī, *m., f.*, day

differtus, -a, -um, *adj.*, stuffed full

difficilis, -e, *adj.*, difficult, troublesome, hard to manage

digitus, -ī, *m.*, finger

dīgredior, dīgredī, dīgressus sum, depart, digress

dīlacerō, dīlacerāre, dīlacerāvī, dīlacerātum, tear to pieces

dīligō, dīligere, dīlexī, dīlectum, love, esteem, hold dear, have special regard for

dīmittō, dīmittere, dīmīsī, dīmissum, let go, send away

Dindymon, -ī, *n.*, Mt. Dindymus, mountain in Phrygia sacred to the goddess Cybele, the Magna Mater, or Great Mother

dīrigō, dīrigere, dīrexī, dīrectum, make straight, direct, mark

dīrus, -a, -um, *adj.*, terrible, awful, dire

discēdō, discēdere, discessī, discessum, go away, depart

discernō, discernere, discrēvī, discrētum, separate, divide

discerpō, discerpere, discerpsī, discerptum, tear to pieces

disertus, -a, -um, *adj.*, skilled in speaking or writing

dispereō, disperīre, disperiī, perish, be destroyed

distinctus, -a, -um, *adj.*, different

dīva, -ae, *f.*, goddess

dīversus, -a, -um, *adj.*, different, from different directions

dīvus, -ī, *m.*, god

dō, dare, dedī, datum, give

doctus, -a, -um, *adj.*, learned, taught

doleō, dolēre, doluī, dolitum, suffer mental or physical pain, be in pain, grieve

dolor, dolōris, *m.*, pain, anguish, grief

domina, -ae, *f.*, female head of a household, mistress, owner

dominus, -ī, *m.*, master, lord, ruler

domō, domāre, domuī, subdue, overcome

domus, -ūs/-ī, *f.*, house, home

dōnō, dōnāre, dōnāvī, dōnātum, present, endow

dōnum, -ī, *n.*, gift

dormiō, dormīre, dormīvī, dormītum, sleep

dubitō, dubitāre, dubitāvī, dubitātum, be in doubt, hesitate

dubius, -a, -um, *adj.*, uncertain, indecisive

dūcō, dūcere, duxī, ductum, lead, take, consider

dulce, *adv.*, sweetly

dulcis, -e, *adj.*, sweet, (of persons) dear, beloved

dum, *conj.*, while, as long as, provided that, if only, until

duo, duae, duo, *adj.*, two

Durrachium, Durrachiī, *n.*, Dyrrachium, town on coast of Illyria

dūrus, -a, -um, *adj.*, hard, harsh

E

ē/ex, *prep. with abl.*, out of, from

ēbrius, -a, -um, *adj.*, drunk

ēdō, ēdere, ēdidī, ēditum, put forth, give out, give birth to, publish

edō, esse, ēdī, ēsum, eat, consume

ēdūcō, ēdūcere, ēduxī, ēductum, lead or bring out, produce

efficiō, efficere, effēcī, effectum, make, bring about, carry out, finish

effigiēs, effigiēī, *f.*, artistic representation, statue, copy

effluō, effluere, effluxī, flow out

ēgelidus, -a, -um, *adj.*, having the chill taken off, tepid

ego, meī, mihi/mī, mē, mē, *pron.*, I, me

ēgredior, ēgredī, ēgressus sum, go or come out, leave

ēgressus, -ūs, *m.*, escape, egress

ēheu, *interj. expressing grief or pain*, alas

ei, *interjection, exclamation expressing anguish*, alas

ēiciō, ēicere, ēiēcī, ēiectum, throw out, expel

ēlectus, -a, -um, *adj.*, selected for excellence, choice

ēlegans, ēlegantis, refined, tastefully attractive, elegant

enim, *conj.*, for, truly

eō, īre, īvī/iī, itum, go

Eōus, -a, -um, *adj.*, connected with the dawn, eastern, oriental

epistolium, epistolī, *n.*, short letter

Erecthēus, -a, -um, *adj.*, of Erectheus, legendary king of Athens; Athenian

Erectheus, Erectheī, *m.*, legendary king of Athens

ēripiō, ēripere, ēripuī, ēreptum, snatch away, rescue

errābundus, -a, -um, *adj.*, wandering

error, errōris, *m.*, wandering about, doubt, mistake, error, delusion

ēruō, ēruere, ēruī, ērutum, uproot, stir up

erus, -ī, *m.*, master

Erycīna, -ae, *f.*, Venus; a temple of Venus was located on Mt. Eryx in Sicily

et, *conj.*, and, even; **et ... et**, both ... and

etiam, *particle*, still, yet, even

etsī, *conj.*, even if, although

Eumenis, Eumenidos, *f.*, one of the Eumenides or Furies who avenge wrongs, sometimes depicted with snakes

Eurōtās, -ae, *m.*, river on which Sparta is located

ēvītō, ēvītāre, ēvītāvī, ēvītātum, avoid

exagitō, exagitāre, exagitāvī, exagitātum, rouse, stir up

exardescō, exardescere, exarsī, catch fire, blaze up

excitō, excitāre, excitāvī, excitātum, rouse, set in motion, excite

excruciō, excruciāre, excruciāvī, excruciātum, torture, torment

excutiō, excutere, excussī, excussum, shake out, drive out, banish

expallescō, expallescere, expalluī, turn pale

expellō, expellere, expulī, expulsum, drive out, expel, banish

explicō, explicāre, explicāvī/explicuī, explicātum/explicitum, unfold, unroll, give an account of

expoliō, expolīre, expolīvī/expoliī, expolītum, smooth down, polish

exposcō, exposcere, expoposcī, ask for, demand, beg

exprimō, exprimere, expressī, expressum, extract, reproduce, copy, translate, express

exprōmō, exprōmere, exprompsī, expromptum, bring out, give expression to, reveal

exsolvō, exsolvere, exsoluī, exsolūtum, set free, release, perform or discharge (a vow or penalty)

exspectō, exspectāre, exspectāvī, exspectātum, wait for, expect, look forward to

exspīrō, exspīrāre, exspīrāvī, exspīrātum, breathe out, emit (odors)

exspuō, exspuere, exspuī, exspūtum, spit out, emit

exsultō, exsultāre, exsultāvī, spring up, behave in an unrestrained manner, run riot, exult

externō/ex(s)ternō, externāre, externāvī, externātum, drive out of one's mind, provoke to panic

extrēmus, -a, -um, *adj.,* situated at the end, edge, or tip; situated at the end of the world, last, final

exturbō, exturbāre, exturbāvī, exturbātum, drive out, banish, disturb

F

fābula, -ae, *f.,* talk, rumor, report, story

Fabullus, -ī, *m.,* Fabullus, friend of Catullus

facētiae, -ārum, *f. pl.,* cleverness, wit

faciō, facere, fēcī, factum, make, do, regard

factum, -ī, *n.,* deed, action

fallax, fallācis, *adj.,* deceitful, deceptive

fallō, fallere, fefellī, falsum, deceive, trick, escape the notice of; *in passive,* be mistaken

falsus, -a, -um, *adj.,* false, faithless, deceitful

famulor, famulārī, famulātus sum, be subject to, be a slave

fās, *indecl. n.,* what is right or allowed by divine law, what is right or proper

fascinō, fascināre, fascināvī, fascinātum, cast a spell on, bewitch

fātum, -ī, *n.,* fate, *pl.,* the Fates

faveō, favēre, fāvī, fautum, favor

fēmina, -ae, *f.,* woman

femur, feminis, *n.,* thigh

fera, -ae, *f.,* wild animal

ferō, ferre, tulī, lātum, bear, bring, carry, tell, claim, play (a part, role)

ferox, ferōcis, *adj.,* bold

ferrūgō, ferrūginis, *f.,* rust, rust color

ferus, -a, -um, *adj.,* wild, uncivilized, cruel

fervidus, -a, -um, *adj.,* boiling, burning, hot, impetuous

fessus, -a, -um, *adj.,* tired, weary

fētus, -ūs, *m.,* begetting, offspring, product of mind or imagination

fidēlis, -e, *adj.,* faithful

fidēs, fideī, *f.,* trust, belief, faith, honesty, honor

fīdus, -a, -um, *adj.,* faithful, loyal

fīgō, fīgere, fīxī, fīxum, drive in, transfix, pierce, fix

figūra, -ae, *f.,* form, shape, figure, image

fīlia, -ae, *f.,* daughter

fīlum, fīlī, *n.,* thread

fīnis, fīnis, *m.,* boundary, limit, end

fīō, fīerī, factus sum, be made, be done, become, happen, occur

flagrans, flagrantis, *adj.,* hot, blazing, passionate

flāmen, flāminis. *n.,* blast, wind, breeze

flamma, -ae, *f.,* flame, fire, burning passion

flāvus, -a, -um, *adj.,* yellow, golden, blonde, auburn

flectō, flectere, flexī, flexum, bend, curve, turn, change, influence

fleō, flēre, flēvī, flētum, weep, weep for, lament

flētus, -ūs, *m.,* weeping, tears, lamentation

flexus, -ūs, *m.,* bending, curve

flōrens, flōrentis, *adj.,* flowering, flourishing, in the flower of one's youth

flōridus, -a, -um, *adj.,* flowery, in the bloom of youth or beauty, blooming

flōs, flōris, *m.,* flower

fluctuō, fluctuāre, fluctuāvī, fluctuātum, undulate, be in turmoil, hesitate

fluctus, -ūs, *m.,* a flowing, wave, disturbance

fluentisonus, -a, -um, *adj.,* resounding with noise of waves

fluitō, fluitāre, fluitāvī, flow, hang loose, float

flūmen, flūminis, *n.,* river, waters of a river

foedō, foedāre, foedāvī, foedātum, make filthy, stain

foedus, foederis, *n.,* treaty, compact

forma, -ae, *f.,* form, appearance, image, beauty

Formiānus, -a, -um, *adj.,* of or belonging to Formiae, city on coast of Latium

formōsus, -a, -um, *adj.,* having a fine appearance, beautiful, handsome

fors, fortis, *f.,* chance, luck

fortasse, *adv.,* perhaps

forte, *adv.,* by chance, as luck would have it, as it so happened

fortūna, -ae, *f.,* fortune, chance, luck

forum, -ī, *n.,* forum, public square in center of a town, Roman Forum

fossor, fossōris, *m.,* ditchdigger, uncouth individual

frangō, frangere, frēgī, fractum, break, crush

frāter, frātris, *m.,* brother

frāternus, -a, -um, *adj.,* brotherly, of or belonging to a brother

frequens, frequentis, *adj.,* crowded, assiduous, constant, regular

fretum, -ī, *n.,* strait, sea

frīgidulus, -a, -um, *adj.,* chilly, cold

frīgidus, -a, -um, cold, lacking energy, feeble

frīgus, frigoris, *n.,* cold, coldness, lukewarm or unfavorable reception, flatness or frigidity of writing style

frondōsus, -a, -um, *adj.,* leafy

frons, frontis, *f.,* forehead, brow, front

frustrā, *adv.,* in vain, to no purpose

frustror, frustrārī, frustrātus sum, delude, escape, elude, evade

fuga, -ae, *f.,* flight, desertion

fugiō, fugere, fūgī, fugitum, flee, flee from, avoid

fugō, fugāre, fugāvī, fugātum, cause to flee, drive away

fulgeō, fulgēre, fulsī, shine brightly, gleam, be bright

fulgor, fulgōris, *m.,* brightness, radiance

funditus, *adv.,* from the bottom, completely

fundō, fundere, fūdī, fūsum, pour, spread, scatter, defeat

fundus, -ī, *m.,* bottom, farm, estate

fūnestō, fūnestāre, fūnestāvī, fūnestātum, pollute by murder, stain with blood, make mournful

fūnestus, -a, -um, *adj.,* of mourning, funereal, deadly

fūnis, fūnis, *m.,* rope, cable, mooring rope

fūnus, fūneris, *n.,* funeral, death, destruction

furens, furentis, *adj.,* mad, wild

Fūrius, Fūrī, *m.,* Furius; may be the poet Furius Bibaculus

furor, furōris, *m.,* madness, frenzy, fury

furtīvus, -a, -um, *adj.,* stolen, secret

furtum, -ī, *n.,* theft, secret action, stolen article

G

Gāius, Gāī, cf. **Cinna**

Gallicus, -a, -um, *adj.,* of Gaul or the Gauls

gaudeō, gaudēre, gāvīsus sum, rejoice, delight in *(with abl.)*

gaudium, gaudī, *n.,* joy, delight

Gellius, Gellī, *m.,* Gellius; addressed by Catullus in a group of sexually abusive epigrams; probably Lucius Gellius Poplicola, who belonged to the circle of Clodia Metelli at the time of Cicero's speech in defense of Caelius (*Pro Caelio*)

gemellus, -a, -um, *adj.,* twin

geminus, -a, -um, *adj.,* twin, double

gemō, gemere, gemuī, gemitum, groan, moan, lament

gener, generī, *m.,* son-in-law

genitor, genitōris, *m.,* father, originator

gens, gentis, *f.,* people, nation, clan, tribe, family

genus, generis, *n.,* birth, race, kind, offspring

germānus, -ī, *m.,* brother

gerō, gerere, gessī, gestum, bear, carry, do

gestiō, gestīre, gestīvī, desire eagerly, be impatient, act without restraint, exult

gignō, gignere, genuī, genitum, give birth to, produce

gnāta, -ae, *f.,* daughter

gnātus, -ī, *m.,* son; *pl.,* children

Golgī, -ōrum, *m. pl.,* town in Cyprus connected with worship of Venus

Gortȳnius, -a, -um, of Gortyn, city on Crete

grabātus, -ī, *m.,* a low, usually cheap, bed or couch

gradior, gradī, gressus sum, step, walk, proceed

grātēs, grātium, *f. pl.,* thanks

grātia, -ae, *f.,* kindness, favor, thanks

grātus, -a, -um, *adj.,* pleasing

gravēdō, gravēdinis, *f.,* head cold, heavy oppressive feeling

gravis, -e, *adj.,* heavy, weighty, serious

gremium, gremī, *n.,* lap, breast, female genital parts

gurges, gurgitis, *m.,* eddy, whirlpool, waters of river or sea

H

habeō, habēre, habuī, habitum, have, hold, consider, keep

habitō, habitāre, habitāvī, habitātum, live in, inhabit

Hadria, -ae, *m.,* the Adriatic Sea

Hadriāticum, -ī, *n.,* the Adriatic Sea

harēna, -ae, *f.,* sand, beach, desert, arena

harundinōsus, -a, -um, *adj.,* full of reeds, reedy

hendecasyllabus, -a, -um, *adj.,* of a line of poetry consisting of eleven syllables; *m. pl.,* poetry composed in the hendecasyllabic meter

hērōs, hērōos, *m.,* hero

hesternus, -a, -um, *adj.,* of yesterday

heu, *interj. expressing grief or pain,* oh, alas

Hibēr, Hibēris, *m.*, an inhabitant of the Iberian peninsula

Hibērī, -ōrum, *m. pl.*, the Iberians or Spaniards

Hibērus, -a, -um, *adj.*, Iberian, Spanish

hīc, *adv.*, here, at this point

hic, haec, hoc, *demonstr. pron. and adj.*, this, the latter

hinc, *adv.*, from here, here

homō, hominis, *m.*, person, human being

hōra, -ae, *f.*, hour, time, season

horreō, horrēre, horruī, bristle, shudder at

horribilis, -e, *adj.*, terrifying, rough, monstrous

horridus, -a, -um, *adj.*, rough, harsh, dreadful

Hortalus, -ī, *m.*, Hortalus; may be the Quintus Hortensius Hortalus who was Cicero's rival in the law courts.

hospes, hospitis, *m.*, guest, visitor, host, stranger

hūc, *adv.*, to here, here, to this place

hymenaeus, -ī, *m.*, wedding, marriage *(usually in pl.)*

Hyrcānī, Hyrcānōrum, *m., pl.* the Hyrcanians, Hyrcani; lived on south shore of the Caspian Sea

I

Iacchus, -ī, *m.*, Bacchus

iaceō, iacēre, iacuī, lie, be in ruins

iaciō, iacere, iēcī, iactum, throw, lay foundations

iactō, iactāre, iactāvī, iactātum, throw, toss, shake up, brag

iam, *adv.*, already, now, even then, even now

iambus, -ī, *m.*, iambus, metrical FOOT of one short syllable followed by one long; *(pl.)* invective written in iambic meter

ibī/ibĭ, *adv.*, there, then

Īdaeus, -a, -um, *adj.*, of Mount Ida on Crete

Īdalium, Īdalī, *n.*, Idalium, town in Cyprus sacred to Venus

īdem, eadem, idem, *pron. and adj.*, the same, too, likewise

identidem, *adv.*, repeatedly, again and again, continually

igitur, *conj.*, therefore, then, so

ignārus, -a, -um, ignorant, unaware

ignis, ignis, *m.*, fire

ignoscō, ignoscere, ignōvī, ignōtum, forgive, pardon

ignōtus, -a, -um, *adj.*, unknown, obscure, ignorant

īlia, īlium, *n. pl.*, side of the body extending from hips to the groin, sometimes used especially to refer to the groin or private parts; "balls"

ille, illa, illud, *demonstr. pron. and adj.*, that, the former

illepidus, -a, -um, *adj.*, lacking grace or refinement

illīc, *adv.*, there

illic, illaec, illuc, *pron., adj.*, that

illinc, *adv.*, from there, from that time

illūc, *adv.*, to that place, there

imbuō, imbuere, imbuī, imbūtum, wet, fill, inspire

immātūrus, -a, -um, *adj.*, unripe, immature, premature, untimely

immemor, immemoris, *adj.*, forgetful, unmindful

immītis, -e, *adj.*, harsh, bitter

immō, *particle correcting previous statement*, rather

impensē, *adv.*, immoderately, excessively

impetus, -ūs, *m.*, attack, onset, rapid motion, violent onward motion or force

impius, -a, -um, *adj.*, impious, undutiful, disloyal

impotens, impotentis, *adj.*, powerless, weak, wild, violent

īmus, -a, -um, *adj.*, lowest, bottom of

in, *prep. with abl.*, in, on; *prep. with acc.*, into, onto, against, over

incendium, incendī, *n.*, fire, fire (of love)

incendō, incendere, incendī, incensum, burn, make hot, inflame, excite

incidō, incidere, incidī, incāsum, fall on, rush on, happen on, present itself in conversation

incitō, incitāre, incitāvī, incitātum, incite, urge on, arouse

incohō, incohāre, incohāvī, incohātum, start working on, begin, establish

incola, -ae, *m., f.*, inhabitant

incommodum, -ī, *n.*, detriment, unfavorable circumstance, affliction

incurvō, incurvāre, incurvāvī, incurvātum, bend, extend in a curve

inde, *adv.*, from that point, from there, from that time, from then, then

India, -ae, *f.*, India, poorly defined region of Asia covering from modern-day India to the borders of China

indicō, indicāre, indicāvī, indicātum, point out, show, declare

indignē, *adv.*, unworthily, undeservedly

indomitus, -a, -um, *adj.*, unconquer-ed, unconquerable, wild

indūcō, indūcere, indūxī, inductum, bring in, entice, lead into a false situation

Indus, -ī, *m.*, an inhabitant of India

ineptiō, ineptīre, play the fool, be silly

ineptus, -a, -um, *adj.*, having no sense of what is fitting, foolish, silly

infacētus, -a, -um, *adj.*, boorish, not witty or smart

infēlix, infēlīcis, *adj.*, unproductive, unlucky, unhappy

inferiae, -ārum, *f. pl.*, rites in honor of the dead; offerings to the dead (wine, milk, honey, flowers etc.)

infestus, -a, -um, *adj.*, dangerous, hostile, insecure

inficētiae, -ārum, *f. pl.*, instances of clumsiness

inficiō, inficere, infēcī, infectum, dye, imbue, taint, stain

infimus, -a, -um, *adj.*, lowest, most humble

infundō, infundere, infūdī, infūsum, pour in, fill

ingenuus, -a, -um, *adj.*, natural, freeborn, generous, befitting a free person

ingrātus, -a, -um, *adj.*, marked by ingratitude, ungrateful, unwelcome, unattractive

inguen, inguinis, *n.*, swelling on groin, groin, sexual organs

iniciō, inicere, iniēcī, iniactum (iniectum), throw in or on, put one's hands on

inīquus, -a, -um, *adj.*, uneven, unfavorable, treacherous, discontented

iniūria, -ae, *f.*, unlawful conduct, unjust act, insult

iniustus, -a, -um, *adj.*, unjust, unfair, lawless

inmerens, inmerentis, *adj.*, undeserving, blameless

innuptus, -a, -um, *adj.*, (of women) unmarried

inobservābilis, -e, *adj.*, difficult to trace or observe

inops, inopis, *adj.*, lacking wealth, poor

inpotens, inpotentis, *adj.*, powerless, weak, wild, violent

inquam, inquit, *defective verb* (only a few forms occur, most often used parenthetically or before or after a quotation), say

insapiens, insapientis, *adj.*, unwise, foolish

insidiae, -ārum, *f. pl.*, ambush, treacherous attack

insula, -ae, *f.*, island, apartment building

insulsus, -a, -um, *adj.*, unsalted, unattractive, boring, dull, stupid

insultō, insultāre, insultāvī, insultātum, leap or trample on, mock

inter, *prep. with acc.*, between, among

intereā, *adv.*, meanwhile

interficiō, interficere, interfēcī, interfectum, kill, destroy

interior, interius, *adj.*, inner, interior, private

interitus, -ūs, *m.*, violent or untimely death; fact or process of being destroyed

intestīnum, -ī, *n.*, alimentary canal, or part of it; *in pl.*, intestines, guts

intortus, -a, -um, *adj.*, twisted, crooked

invenustus, -a, -um, *adj.*, lacking in charm or beauty, unlovely, unattractive

invictus, -a, -um, *adj.*, unconquered, invincible

invideō, invidēre, invīdī, invīsum, envy, begrudge, refuse

invīsō, invīsere, invīsī, invīsum, go to see, visit, have visual experience of, see

invītus, -a, -um, *adj.*, unwilling, reluctant, not wishing

iocor, iocārī, iocātus sum, joke

iocōsē, *adv.*, humorously, playfully

iocōsus, -a, -um, *adj.*, full of fun, full of joking

iocus, -ī, *m.*, joke, jest, joking

Īonius, -a, -um, *adj.*, Ionian, related to the Ionian Sea, west of Greece

ipse, ipsa, ipsum, *pron., adj.*, himself, herself, itself, oneself, etc.

īra, -ae, *f.*, anger, wrath, rage

irritus, -a, -um, made null and void, empty

irrumātor, irrumātōris, *m.*, a man who forces someone to give him oral sex; METAPHORICALLY, one who treats another with contempt

is, ea, id, *pron. and adj.*, he, she, it, this, that

iste, ista, istud, *pron. and adj.*, that of yours, this, that (*often with derogatory sense*)

istinc, *adv.*, from there

ita, *adv.*, thus, so

Italus, -a, -um, *adj.*, Italian

iter, itineris, *n.*, journey

Itōnus, Itōnī, *f.*, name of Thessalian and Boeotian towns associated with Athena

Itylus, -ī, *m.*, Itylus; here, son of Procne and Tereus; known as Itys in other versions

iubeō, iubēre, iussī, iussum, order, command, bid

iūcundus, -a, -um, *adj.*, delightful, agreeable

iugum, -ī, *n.*, yoke, bond, ridge, chariot

Iuppiter, Iovis, *m.*, Jupiter, supreme god of the Romans, god of sky and weather

iūrō, iūrāre, iūrāvī, iūrātum, swear, vow, affirm

iustus, -a, -um, lawful, fair, just

iuvenis, iuvenis, *m., f.*, young man, young woman

iuvō, iuvāre, iūvī, iūtum, please, delight, help

L

labefactō, labefactāre, labefactāvī, labefactātum, loosen, cause to waver, shake (someone's resolve)

labellum, -ī, *n.*, lip

labor, labōris, *m.*, work, effort, task

labōriōsus, -a, -um, involving much work, toilsome, industrious

labyrinthēus, -a, -um, *adj.*, labyrinthine

lacrima, -ae, *f.*, tear, lament

lactens, lactentis, *adj.*, full of milk, milk-white

lacus, lacūs, *m.*, lake, pond, pool

laedō, laedere, laesī, laesum, harm, strike

laetitia, -ae, *f.*, happiness, joy

laetor, laetārī, laetātus sum, rejoice, delight in

laetus, -a, -um, *adj.*, happy, glad, fertile

laevus, -a, -um, *adj.*, left, unfavorable, coming from the left

langueō, languēre, be sluggish, languid, weak

languescō, languescere, languī, grow weak

languidus, -a, -um, *adj.*, languid, sluggish, slow

lapis, lapidis, *m.*, stone

lar, laris, *m.*, one of a class of Roman gods associated with protection of places; tutelary god of hearth or home; home

Lārius, -a, -um, *adj.*, of Lake Larius in Cisalpine Gaul, Lago di Como (Lake Como)

lāsarpīcifer, lāsarpīcifera, lāsarpīciferum, *adj.*, silphium-bearing

lātē, *adv.*, widely, over a large area

lātrō, lātrāre, lātrāvī, lātrātum, bark, roar

lātus, -a, -um, adj, wide

laus, laudis, *f.*, praise

leaena, -ae, *f.*, lioness

lectīca, -ae, *f.*, litter

lectulus, -ī, *m.*, couch, bed (also used for reclining at meals or studying)

lectus, -i, *m.*, bed, couch (also used for reclining at meals or studying)

legō, legere, lēgī, lectum, gather, collect, read, recite

lēniō, lēnīre, lēnīvī, lēnītum, assuage, placate, calm, explain away

lēnis, -e, *adj.*, smooth, gentle, mild, soft

lēniter, *adv.*, gently, without aspiration

lentus, -a, -um, *adj.*, slow, lingering, unresponsive, pliant

leō, leōnis, *m.*, lion

lepidē, *adv.*, charmingly, delightfully, wittily, amusingly

lepidus, -a, -um, *adj.*, charming, delightful, witty, amusing

lepos, lepōris, *m.*, charm, grace, attractiveness, wit

Lesbia, -ae, *f.*, Lesbia; pseudonym in the poems for Catullus' beloved (see Introduction)

Lēthaeus, -a, -um, *adj.*, of Lethe, the river in the underworld that produces oblivion; causing sleep or forgetfulness

levis, -e, *adj.*, light, swift, gentle, unimportant, fickle

leviter, *adv.*, lightly, gently, quietly

levō, levāre, levāvī, levātum, lift, remove, relieve

libellus, -ī, *m.*, a small work written for publication, volume, little book

libenter, *adv.*, with pleasure, willingly, gladly

līber, lībera, līberum, *adj.*, free

liber, librī, *m.*, inner bark of a tree, book, volume, roll

libīdō, libīdinis, *f.*, desire, longing, sexual desire, lust; *in pl.*, instance of desire

librārius, librārī, *m.*, scribe, bookseller, secretary

Libya, -ae, *f.*, Libya, general term for whole of North Africa

Libyssa, -ae, *f. adj.*, Libyan, of north Africa, African

Libystīnus, -a, -um, *adj.*, African

licet, licēre, licuit/licitum est, *impers.*, it is permitted

Licinius, Licinī. *m.*, Gaius Licinius Calvus, 82–47 BCE, intimate friend of Catullus; poet, orator

lignum, -ī, *n.*, wood; *especially pl.*, firewood

ligō, ligāre, ligāvī, ligātum, fasten, bind

līmen, līminis, *n.*, threshold

limpidus, -a, -um, *adj.*, clear, transparent

lingua, -ae, *f.*, tongue, language

linquō, linquere, līquī, go away from, abandon, leave behind

linteum, -ī, *n.*, piece of linen cloth, sail, towel, napkin, curtain

liqueō, liquēre, licuī/liquī, be liquid, be clear, appear clear

liquidus, -a, -um, *adj.*, flowing, clear, melodious, liquid

lītorālis, lītorāle, *adj.*, of the seashore, of the shore

litterātor, litterātōris, *m.*, elementary school teacher

lītus, lītoris, *n.*, shore, coast, beach

locō, locāre, locāvī, locātum, place, station

longē, *adv.*, far, far off, far away in time, by far

longus, -a, -um, *adj.*, long

loquor, loquī, locūtus sum, speak

lōrum, -ī, *n.*, leather strap; *pl.*, horse's reins

lubet (libet), lubēre, libuit/libitum est, *impers.*, it is pleasing or agreeable

lūceō, lūcēre, luxī, shine, dawn, become light

luctus, -ūs, *m.*, expression of grief, mourning

lūdō, lūdere, lūsī, lūsum, play, amuse oneself, play sexually, write light poetry

lūgeō, lūgēre, luxī, luctum, mourn, lament

lūmen, lūminis, *n.*, light, day, eye, glory

lux, lūcis, *f.*, light, daylight, day, life

Lȳdius, -a, -um, *adj.*, Lydian, Etruscan

lympha, -ae, *f.*, water

M

maeror, maerōris, *m.*, grief, mourning

maestus, -a, -um, *adj.*, sad, sorrowful, dejected, gloomy

magis, *adv.*, more, more nearly

magnanimus, -a, -um, *adj.*, brave, bold

magnus, -a, -um, *adj.*, large, big, great

maior, maius, *adj.*, greater, larger

male, *adv.*, badly, insufficiently, wickedly, scarcely, awfully

malignē, *adv.*, poorly, insufficiently

malignus, -a, -um, *adj.*, ungenerous, unkind

mālō, mālle, māluī, prefer

mālum, -ī, *n.*, originally, most soft-skinned tree fruit, later, normally specifying an apple

malum, -ī, *n.*, trouble, distress, misfortune, evil, harm

malus, -a, -um, *adj.*, bad, nasty, hostile, unfavorable

mālus, -ī, *m.*, pole, beam, mast of a ship

mandātum, -ī, *n.*, order, instruction

maneō, manēre, mansī, mansum, remain, stay, endure, stop, await

Manlius, Manlī, *m.*, Manlius; otherwise unknown

mānō, mānāre, mānāvī, mānātum, flow, spread

mantica, -ae, *f.*, knapsack, pack

manus, -ūs, *f.*, hand, band

Marcus Tullius Cicerō, Marcī Tullī Cicerōnis, Roman orator, writer, statesman; 106–43 BCE

mare, maris, *n.*, sea

Marrūcīnus, -a, -um, *adj.*, of or belonging to the Marrucini, a people living on the east coast of central Italy

māter, mātris, *f.*, mother

māternus, -a, -um, *adj.*, maternal

maximus, -a, -um, *adj.*, biggest, largest, oldest, greatest

medius, -a, -um, *adj.*, middle

medulla, -ae, *f.*, bone marrow, one's interior, heart or mind (as seat of deep thought and emotion)

melior, melius, *adj.*, better

mellītus, -a, -um. *adj.*, honeyed, delightful as honey, honey-sweet

membrāna, -ae, *f.*, membrane, covering, parchment (the skin of sheep, goats, etc. prepared for use as a writing material), parchment used as a cover for manuscripts

membrum, -ī, *n.*, limb or member of the body, limb, member, part of anything

meminī, meminisse, perf. with pres. meaning; remember, recollect

memor, memoris, *adj.*, mindful, remembering

mens, mentis, *f.*, mind

mersō, mersāre, mersāvī, mersātum, dip, submerge, drown, overwhelm

merus, -a, -um, *adj.*, pure, unmixed

metuō, metuere, metuī, metūtum, fear, be afraid of, be afraid

meus, -a, -um, *adj.*, my

mīca, -ae, *f.*, grain, particle, crumb

micō, micāre, micuī, quiver, dart, flash

mīliēs, *adv.*, a thousand times (often HYPERBOLIC)

mille, *indecl. n. and adj.*, a thousand; *pl.*, **mīlia**

minax, minācis, *adj.*, threatening, projecting

minimus, -a, -um, *adj.*, smallest, least

Mīnōis, Mīnōidis, *f.*, female descendant of Minos; Ariadne

Mīnōs, Mīnōis/Minōnis, *m.*, Minos, king of Crete, and later a judge in the underworld; **Mīnōa** *(accusative singular)*

Mīnōtaurus, -ī, *m.*, the Minotaur; half-man, half-bull born from the union of Pasiphae and a bull, housed in the Labyrinth and killed by Theseus

minus, *adv.*, less

mīrificē, *adv.*, amazingly, remarkably

mīror, mīrārī, mīrātus sum, be surprised, wonder at, admire

mīrus, -a, -um, *adj.*, amazing, extraordinary

misceō, miscēre, miscuī, mixtum, mix, mingle

misellus, -a, -um, *adj.*, wretched, pitiable, unfortunate

miser, misera, miserum, *adj.*, unhappy, pitiful

miserē, *adv.*, wretchedly, desperately

misereor, miserērī, miseritum, pity, feel or show compassion

miserescō, miserescere, have compassion for *(with gen.)*

mitra, -ae, *f.*, Oriental headdress tied with ribbons under chin

mittō, mittere, mīsī, missum, release, let go, abandon, send

mnēmosynum, -ī, *n.*, souvenir, keepsake

modo, *adv.*, only, just now; **modo . . . modo**, now . . . now

modus, -ī, *m.*, limit, way, rhythmic pattern; *pl.*, poetry

moechus, -ī, *m.*, adulterer, man who pursues inappropriate women

moenia, -ium, *n. pl.*, defensive walls of a town or city, town or city enclosed by walls

molestus, -a, -um, *adj.*, troublesome, annoying, tiresome

mollis, -e, *adj.*, soft, gentle, flexible, voluptuous

monimentum, -ī, *n.*, monument, memorial

mons, montis, *m.*, mountain

monstrum, -ī, *n.*, portent, marvel, monster

morbus, -ī, *m.*, sickness, disease

mordeō, mordēre, momordī, morsum, bite, nibble, gnaw

morior, morī, mortuus sum, die

moror, morārī, morātus sum, delay, linger, be late in appearing

mors, mortis, *f.*, death

morsus, morsūs, *m.*, bite

mortālis, -e, *adj.*, mortal

mōs, mōris, *m.*, custom, tradition; *pl.* character, habits

mōtus, -ūs, *m.*, motion, movement, passion, upheaval

moveō, movēre, mōvī, mōtum, move

mulier, mulieris, *f.*, woman, wife

multa, -ae, *f.*, fine, penalty

multiplex, multiplicis, *adj.*, having many twists or turns, multitudinous, varied

multō, *adv.*, by far, by much

multō, multāre, multāvī, multātum, fine, punish

multum, *adv.*, much

multus, -a, -um, much, many, large

mundus, -ī, *m.*, sky, world

mūnus, mūneris, *n.*, service, duty, gift, entertainment, offering

mūnusculum, -ī, *n.*, little gift

mūsa, -ae, *f.*, muse; one of the nine Muses, goddesses who were daughters of Zeus and Mnemosyne and presided over the arts

mūtō, mūtāre, mūtāvī, mūtātum, change, exchange

mūtus, -a, -um, *adj.*, inarticulate, dumb, silent, mute

mūtuus, -a, -um, *adj.*, mutual, reciprocal; *n. pl. with adverbial force*, reciprocally, mutually

myrtus, -ī/ūs, *f.*, myrtle

N

nam, *conj.*, for, because

namque, *conj.*, for, because

narrō, narrāre, narrāvī, narrātum, tell, say

nascor, nascī, nātus sum, be born

nāsus, -ī, *m.*, nose

natō, natāre, natāvī, natātum, swim, float, hover

naufragus, -a, -um, *adj.*, shipwrecked, shipwrecking

nāvis, nāvis, *f.*, ship

nāvita, -ae, *m.*, sailor

-ne, *enclitic interrogative particle*; occasionally, *affirmative particle*

nē, negative *adv.*, and *conj.*, not, that not, so that not, lest; used in negative purpose clauses and prohibitions, among other constructions

nebula, -ae, *f.*, mist, fog

nec, *conj.*, and not; **nec . . . nec**, neither . . . nor

necdum, *conj. and adv.*, (and) not yet

necesse, *adv.*, necessary

nefārius, -a, -um, *adj.*, offending against moral law, evil, horrible

neglectus, -a, -um, *adj.*, not cared for, neglected

neglegens, neglegentis, *adj.*, careless, untidy, neglectful

neglegō, neglegere, neglexī, neglectum, be indifferent to, neglect

negō, negāre, negāvī, negātum, say no, deny, refuse

Nemesis, Nemeseōs, *f.*, Nemesis, Greek goddess of retribution

nepōs, nepōtis, *m., f.*, grandchild, descendant

Neptūnus, -ī, *m.*, Neptune, Roman god of the sea.

neque, *conj.*, and not; **neque . . . neque**, neither . . . nor

nequeō, nequīre, nequīvī/nequiī, be unable

nēquīquam, *adv.*, to no effect, in vain

nesciō, nescīre, nescīvī, nescītum, not know, be ignorant of, not to know how to, not to be able to

nescio quis, nescio quid, *indefinite pron. or adj.*, someone or other, something or other

nescius, -a, -um, *adj.*, ignorant, unaware

neu, *conj.*, and that . . . not

nī, nisi, *conj.*, if not, unless

Nīcaea, -ae, *f.*, Nicaea, city in Bithynia

niger, nigra, nigrum, *adj.*, black, dark, gloomy, black as a color of ill omen, evil

nihil, *n., indecl.*, nothing

Nīlus, -ī, *m.*, the river Nile

nīmīrum, *particle*, without doubt, of course

nimis, *adv.*, very, too much, too

nimium, *adv.*, too, too much, very

niteō, nitēre, nituī, shine, be radiant with beauty

nītor, nītī, nixus sum, lean, struggle, strive, rely on

niveus, -a, -um, *adj.*, snowy, snow-white

nōbilis, -e, *adj.*, noble

nōlō, nōlle, nōluī, not want, be unwilling, refuse

nōn, *adv.*, not

nōndum, *adv.*, not yet

nōs, nostrī/nostrum, nōbīs, nōs, nōbīs, *pron.*, we, us

noscō, noscere, nōvī, nōtum, get to know, learn; know *(in perfect tense)*

noster, nostra, nostrum, *adj.*, our

nota, -ae, *f.*, mark, sign, wine of a specified quality or vintage, class, character

nōtus, -a, -um, *adj.*, known, familiar

novissimus, -a, -um, *adj.*, recent, latest, last, most extreme, greatest, *adv.*, very recently

Novum Comum, Novī Comī, *n.*, New Comum, modern Como

novus, -a, -um, *adj.*, new, strange

nox, noctis, *f.*, night

nūbēs, nūbis, *f.*, cloud

nūbō, nūbere, nūpsī, nūptum, marry (typically with woman as the subject)

nūdō, nūdāre, nūdāvī, nūdātum, make naked, strip, uncover

nūgae, nūgārum, *f. pl.*, things not serious, nonsense, worthless stuff

nullus, -a, -um, *adj.*, no, not any; *adverbially*, not at all

num, *interr. particle*, certainly not

nūmen, nūminis, *n.*, nod, divine power, divinity, god

numerus, -ī, *m.*, number, poetic meter

numquam, *adv.*, never

nunc, *adv.*, now

nuntiō, nuntiāre, nuntiāvī, nuntiātum, bring word of, announce

nuntius, nuntī, *m.*, messenger, message

nūper, *adv.*, recently

Nȳsigena, -ae, *m., adj.*, born on legendary Mount Nysa, birthplace of Bacchus

O

ō, *interj.*, O *(with voc.)*

obdūrō, obdūrāre, obdūrāvī, obdūrātum, be persistent, hold out, endure

oblectō, oblectāre, oblectāvī, oblectātum, delight, amuse, entertain

oblītterō, oblīterrāre, oblīttāvī, oblīterrātum, cause to be forgotten, efface

oblīviscor, oblīviscī, oblītus sum, forget

obscurō, obscurāre, obscurāvī, obscurātum, obscure, darken, hide

obstinātus, -a, -um, *adj.*, resolute, stubborn, obstinate

obterō, obterere, obtrīvī, obtrītum, crush, trample underfoot

obvius, -a, -um, *adj. (with dat.)*, in the way, placed so as to meet, situated so as to confront

occidō, occidere, occidī, occāsum, fall, die

ocellus, -ī, *m.*, a little eye; as term of endearment, darling

octo, *indecl. adj.*, eight

oculus, -ī, *m.*, eye

ōdī, ōdisse, ōsum, *perfect with present sense*, have an aversion to, hate

odium, odī, *n.*, hatred, dislike

odor, odōris, *m.*, smell, odor, perfume

offerō, offerre, obtulī, oblātum, show, provide, cause

officium, officī, *n.*, service, duty, function, office

offirmō, offirmāre, offirmāvī, offirmātum, make firm, make up one's mind not to yield

olfaciō, olfacere, olfēcī, olfactum, smell

ōlim, *adv.*, formerly, once, on an occasion, at some future date

omnipotens, omnipotentis, *adj.*, all powerful

omnis, -e, *adj.*, all, every

onus, oneris, *n.*, burden

opera, -ae, *f.*, effort

oportet, oportēre, oportuit, *impers.*, it is right, proper

opprimō, opprimere, oppressī, oppressum, press on, overwhelm, oppress

ops, opis, *f.*, power, aid, assistance

optimus, -a, -um, *adj.*, best, very good

optō, optāre, optāvī, optātum, desire, choose

opus, operis, *n.*, work, business, task, genre; with **esse**, be necessary, be needed

ōrāclum, -ī, *n.*, oracle

ōrātiō, ōrātiōnis, *f.*, act of speaking, language, speech, oration

Orcus, Orcī, *m.*, Orcus, the god of the lower world, the lower world, death

orīgō, orīginis, *f.*, beginning, birth, starting point, source

ōrō, ōrāre, ōrāvī, ōrātum, plead, beg, beseech

ōs, ōris, *n.*, mouth, words, face

ostendō, ostendere, ostendī, ostentum, show, display, indicate

ostentō, ostentāre, ostentāvī, ostentātum, display, show, indicate

ōtiōsus, -a, -um, *adj.*, not occupied by business, at leisure, idle

ōtium, ōtī, *n.*, free time, leisure, peace

P

paene, *adv.*, almost

paeniteō, paenitēre, paenituī, regret

palimpsestum, -ī, *n.*, a palimpsest; Greek loan word, literally "scraped again," papyrus or parchment writing material that is scraped or washed and reused for more writing

pallidulus, -a, -um, *adj.*, pale

palmula, -ae, *f.*, front of the hand, palm, oar

papilla, -ae, *f.*, nipple; here, more generally, breast

papȳrus, -ī, *f.*, papyrus; plant found in Egypt or writing material made from the plant

pār, paris, *adj.*, equal, well-matched, fitting

parātus, -a, -um, *adj.*, prepared

parcō, parcere, pepercī, parsum, spare *(with dat.)*

parens, parentis, *m., f.*, parent, father or mother; *pl.*, parents; *(usually in pl.)* ancestor, originator

parō, parāre, parāvī, parātum, prepare, buy, get

pars, partis, *f.*, part, party; stage role *(usually in pl.)*, part, unit in explaining a fraction (math.)

Parthī, Parthōrum, *m., pl.* Parthians; eastern people hostile to Rome whose kingdom extended from the Euphrates to the Indus rivers

passer, passeris *m.*, a small bird, usually taken to be a sparrow, but sometimes a blue thrush

passim, *adv.*, here and there

pateō, patēre, patuī, be open

pater, patris, *m.*, father

patior, patī, passus sum, suffer, undergo, experience, endure, allow

patrius, -a, -um, *adj.*, of a father, ancestral, native, inherited, belonging to one's country

patrōna, -ae, *f.*, protector, patron; feminine alternative to **patrōnus**

patrōnus, -ī, *m.*, patron, former master of a freed slave, one who pleads for a client in court, advocate

paucus, -a, -um, *adj.*, in pl., few

paulum, *adv.*, for a short while

peccātum, -ī, *n.*, error, mistake, moral offense

pectus, pectoris, *n.*, breast, chest, heart

pelagus, -ī, *n.*, sea

pellō, pellere, pepulī, pulsum, push, drive, strike

penātēs, penātium, *m. pl.*, guardian gods of the Roman pantry considered to control the destiny of the household, these gods in their material form as images, one's home

pendeō, pendēre, pependī, hang, hang down, be suspended

penetrō, penetrāre, penetrāvī, penetrātum, penetrate, make one's way into or as far as

per, *prep. with acc.*, through, according to, as far as __ is concerned

perditē, *adv.*, to desperation

perdō, perdere, perdidī, perditum, destroy, lose

perdūcō, perdūcere, perduxī, perductum, conduct, convey, lead

peregrīnus, -a, -um, *adj.*, foreign, alien, situated abroad

perennis, -e, *adj.*, lasting throughout the year, lasting for many years, enduring

pereō, perīre, periī, peritum, perish, die

perferō, perferre, pertulī, perlātum, endure, carry through to the end

perfidus, -a, -um, *adj.*, treacherous, false, deceitful

perhibeō, perhibēre, perhibuī, perhibitum, present, tell

periūrium, periūrī, *n.*, false oath, perjury

perlūcidulus, -a, -um, *adj.*, transparent, translucent

permulceō, permulcēre, permulsī, permulsum, stroke, soothe, charm

perniciēs, perniciēī, *f.*, physical destruction, fatal injury, ruin, undoing, source of destruction

pernumerō, pernumerāre, pernumerāvī, pernumerātum, count up

perpetior, perpetī, perpessus sum, undergo completely, allow

perpetuus, -a, -um, *adj.*, continuing, permanent, connected

perscrībō, perscrībere, perscripsī, perscriptum, write out fully

perspiciō, perspicere, perspexī, perspectum, look over thoroughly, survey, study, recognize, become aware of

perūrō, perūrere, perussī, perustum, burn up, consume

perveniō, pervenīre, pervēnī, perventum arrive at, reach

pervigilō, pervigilāre, pervigilāvī, pervigilātum, stay awake all night or for a particular period, keep watch all night

pervincō, pervincere, pervīcī, pervictum, overcome, gain

pēs, pedis, *m.*, foot, metrical FOOT, a leg or foot of an article of furniture; nautical term, sheet, the rope by which the lower two corners of a sail are attached to a ship

pessimus, -a, -um, *adj.*, worst, very bad

pestilentia, -ae, *f.*, plague, pestilence

pestis, pestis, *f.*, physical destruction or death, plague, pest

petītor, petītōris, *m.*, seeker, candidate

petō, petere, petīvī, petītum, seek, go after, attack

phasēlus, -ī, *m.*, *f.*, kind of bean, light ship

Phrygius, -a, -um, *adj.*, Phrygian

pietās, pietātis, *f.*, duty, devotion

pignus, pigneris/pignoris, *n.*, pledge, token, symbol, stake

pilus, -ī, *m.*, a hair, something of minimal size or value

pīnus, -ūs, *f.*, pine

pīpiō, pīpiāre, chirp

Pīraeus, Pīraeī, *m.*, Piraeus, port of Athens

pius, -a, -um, *adj.*, dutiful, devoted

placeō, placēre, placuī, placitum, please

plēnus, -a, -um, *adj.*, full

plumbum, -ī, *n.*, lead; lead used for drawing lines

plūrimum, *adv.*, to the greatest extent

plūrimus, -a, -um, *adj.*, very many, most

plūs, *adv.*, more

plūs, plūris, *n.*, more; **plūrēs, plūra**, *pl. adj.*, more

poēma, poēmatis, *n.*, poem

poena, -ae, *f.*, penalty paid for an offense, punishment, revenge

poēta, -ae, *m.*, poet

Polliō, Polliōnis, *m.*, Gaius Asinius Pollio, 76 BCE—4 CE, politician and writer, historian of the civil wars; friend of Catullus, Horace, Vergil

pōnō, pōnere, posuī, positum, put, place, provide, supply

Ponticus, -a, -um, *adj.*, Pontic, of the Black Sea or the region adjoining it

pontus, -ī, *m.*, sea

porrō, *adv.*, forward, further

portō, portāre, portāvī, portātum, carry

portus, -ūs, *m.*, harbor, port, refuge

possum, posse, potuī, be able, can

post, *adv.*, behind, at a later time, afterward; *prep. with acc.*, behind, after

posthāc, *adv.*, from now on, hereafter

postillā, *adv.*, afterwards

postmodo, *adv.*, later, presently

postquam, *conj.*, after

postrēmus, -a, -um, *adj.*, last, latest, final

potis, pote, *indecl. adj.*, able

potius, *adv.*, rather, more (than)

prae, *prep. with abl.*, before, in comparison with

praeceps, praecipitis, *adj.*, headlong, rushing forward

praeceptum, -ī, *n.*, precept, rule

praecingō, praecingere, praecinxī, praecinctum, encircle, gird

praeda, -ae, *f.*, booty, prey, prize

praegestiō, praegestīre, be very eager

praemium, praemī, *n.*, prize, reward

praeportō, praeportāre, carry in front

praeruptus, -a, -um, *adj.*, abrupt, broken off, precipitous, very steep

praesertim, *adv.*, especially

praestō, *adv.*, ready, available

praftereā, *adv.*, besides, moreoever

praftereō, praeterīre, praeteriī, praeteritum, go by, go past, pass by, go beyond, omit

praetor, praetōris, *m.*, praetor; propraetor or governor in charge of running the province

praetrepidō, praetrepidāre, tremble in anticipation

prātum, -ī, *n.*, meadow

pretium, pretī, *n.*, reward, prize, penalty, price, value, cost

prex, precis, *f.*, prayer

prīmum, *adv.*, first

prīmus, -a, -um, *adj.*, first

prior, prius, *adj.*, earlier

priscus, -a, -um, *adj.*, ancient, former

prius, *adv.*, previously, before

prō, *prep. with abl.*, for, on behalf of, in front of, in return for, in payment for

probē, *adv.*, correctly, well

procella, -ae, *f.*, storm, trouble

prōcreō, prōcreāre, prōcreāvī, prōcreātum, create, produce

procul, *adv.*, apart, far away

prōcurrō, prōcurrere, prōcurrī, prōcursum, run forward

prōdō, prōdere, prōdidī, prōditum, project, assert, transmit, betray

prōferō, prōferre, prōtulī, prōlātum, bring forth, utter

proficiscor, proficiscī, profectus sum, start on a journey, set out

profundō, profundere, profūdī, profūsum, pour out, emit

prōiciō, prōicere, prōiēcī, prōiectum, throw forward, give up, abandon

prōmittō, prōmittere, prōmīsī, prōmissum, send forth, let loose, undertake, promise

prōnus, -a, -um, *adj.*, leaning forward, prone, sloping

prope, *adv.*, almost

prōpōnō, prōpōnere, prōposuī, prōpositum, offer, propose, hold out

Propontis, Propontidis/Propontidos, *f.*, the Propontis or Sea of Marmora, between the Aegean Sea and the Black Sea

prōsiliō, prōsilīre, prōsiluī, leap forward, rush forward

prospectō, prospectāre, prospectāvī, prospectātum, gaze out at, look intently at, watch

prospectus, -ūs, *m.*, view, prospect

prosperus, -a, -um, *adj.*, prosperous, successful, favorable

prospiciō, prospicere, prospexī, prospectum, see in front, watch, anticipate

prosternō, prosternere, prostrāvī, prostrātum, lay low, overthrow

prōsum, prōdesse, prōfuī, to be of use, to be beneficial (*with dat.*)

prōtendō, prōtendere, prōtendī, prōtentum, stretch out, extend

prōvincia, -ae, *f.*, province, territory outside Italy under the administration of a Roman governor

pudīcus, -a, -um, *adj.*, having a sense of modesty or shame, modest, honorable, chaste

puella, -ae, *f.*, girl, young woman, girlfriend

puer, puerī, *m.*, boy, non-adult male, male beloved, (young) male slave

pulc(h)er, pulc(h)ra, pulc(h)rum, *adj.*, beautiful, lovely, aesthetically pleasing

pulvis, pulveris, *m.*, dust

pūmex, pūmicis, *m., f.*, pumice or any similar volcanic rock or piece of it

puppis, puppis, *f.*, stern of boat, boat, ship

pūriter, *adv.*, righteously, in a clean manner

purpureus, -a, -um, *adj.*, purple, radiant, glowing

pūrus, -a, -um, *adj.*, clean, pure, plain, chaste

putō, putāre, putāvī, putātum, think, consider, discuss

Q

quā, *indef. adv.*, in any way

quaerō, quaerere, quaesīvī, quaesītum, look for, seek, ask, acquire, earn

quaesō, (quaesere), seek, ask for; first person parenthetically, please

quālis, -e, *rel. adj.*, of which sort, such as

quāliscumque, quālecumque, *rel. adj.*, of whatever sort

quālubet, *adv.*, by any road that pleases, no matter how

quam, *interr. and rel. adv.*, how, as; with the superlative, as . . . as possible; after a comparative, than

quamvīs, *rel. adv.*, to any degree you like, ever so, however, although

quandō, *indef. adv.*, ever

quandōquidem, *rel. adv.*, since, seeing that

quantum, quantī, *n.*, which amount, how much

quantum, *rel. adv.*, to what degree, to what extent

quantus, -a, -um, *adj., interr. and rel. adj.*, how great, of what size

quārē, *interr. and rel. adv.*, in what way, how, why, because, therefore, in this way

quasi, *conj.*, as if

quassō, quassāre, quassāvī, quassātum, shake repeatedly, cause to tremble violently

quatiō, quatere, quassum, shake, beat upon

-que, *enclitic conj.*, and

queō, quīre, quīvī, be able

quercus, -ūs, *f.*, oak tree

querella, -ae, *f.*, complaint, expression of grievance

questus, -ūs, *m.*, complaint, lament

quī, *interr. adv.*, how, in what way

quī, quae, quod, *rel. pron.*, who, which, that; *interr. adj.*, what, which

quī, quae/qua, quod, *indef. adj.* (after **sī**), any

quia, *conj.*, because

quīcumque, quaecumque, quodcumque, *indef. pron.*, whoever, whichever, whatever

quid, *adv.*, why

quīdam, quaedam, quiddam, *pron.*, a certain person, a certain thing

quiēs, quiētis, *f.*, rest, repose, calm, rest of sleep or death

quīn, *adv.*, why not, indeed, but; *conj.*, so that . . . not, but that

quīnam, quaenam, quodnam, *interr. adj.*, + **nam**, what (which) __, tell me?

Quintia, -ae, *f.*, Quintia, woman's name

Quintilia, -ae, *f.*, Quintilia; wife or girlfriend of Calvus

quis, quid, *interr. pron.*, who, what; *indef. pron.*, anyone, anything

quisquam, quicquam, *pron.*, anyone, anything

quisque, quaeque, quidque, *pron.*, each one

quisquis, quidquid/ quicquid, *pron. and adj.*, whoever, whatever

quīvīs, quaevīs, quidvīs, *adj. and pron.*, whatever person or thing you please, anyone, anything

quīvīs cumque, quaevīs cumque, quodvīs cumque, *adj.*, every conceivable, no matter what

quō, *adv.*, where, for what purpose

quod, *conj.*, because

quondam, *adv.*, once, formerly, sometimes, in the future

quoniam, *conj.*, since

quoque, *adv.*, also, too

quot, *indecl. adj.*, how many, as many as

R

rādīcitus, *adv.*, by the roots, completely

ramus, rāmī, *m.*, branch

rapax, rapācis, *adj.*, rapacious, very greedy

rapidus, -a, -um, *adj.*, rapid, violent

rārus, -a, -um, *adj.*, loosely woven, having an open texture, spaced apart, rare

ratiō, ratiōnis, *f.*, calculation, reason, method

ratis, ratis, *f.*, raft, boat, ship

Ravidus, -ī, *m.*, Ravidus; a man's name; otherwise unknown; (read in some texts as Raudus)

recipiō, recipere, recēpī, receptum, take back, accept, regain

reconditus, -a, -um, *adj.*, concealed, secret, secluded

recordor, recordārī, recordātus, recollect, remember

rector, rectōris, *m.*, helmsman, ruler

rectus, -a, -um, *adj.*, straight, right, correct, proper, erect in bearing

recūrō, recūrāre, recūrāvī, recūrātum, cure, restore a thing to its former condition

reddō, reddere, reddidī, redditum, give back, deliver

redeō, redīre, rediī, reditum, go back, come back, return

redimiō, redimīre, redimiī, redimītum, encircle with a garland, surround

redūcō, redūcere, reduxī, reductum, bring back

redux, reducis, *adj.*, that brings back home, returning

referō, referre, retulī, relātum, bring back or again, carry home, render

reficiō, reficere, refēcī, refectum, make again, repair, renew

reflectō, reflectere, reflexī, reflexum, bend back, turn back

rēgius, -a, -um, *adj.*, royal, splendid; technical term used of high quality writing material

regō, regere, rexī, rectum, guide, direct, rule

religō, religāre, religāvī, religātum, tie, fasten behind; occasionally, untie

relinquō, relinquere, relīquī, relictum, leave, leave behind, abandon

remittō, remittere, remīsī, remissum, send back, return, let go, abandon

remūneror, remūnerārī, remūnerātus sum, repay, reward, pay back

rēmus, -ī, *m.*, oar

renovō, renovāre, renovāvī, renovātum, renew, restore, revive

repente, *adv.*, suddenly, in an instant

reperiō, reperīre, repperī, repertum, discover, get, find to be, devise

repōnō, repōnere, reposuī, repositum, put back, put down

reportō, reportāre, reportāvī, reportātum, bring back, carry back

reposcō, reposcere, demand back, demand

requiescō, requiescere, requiēvī, requiētum, rest, be given a rest, relax

requīrō, requīrere, requīsīvī/requīsiī, requīsītum, look for, ask about, try to bring back, need, miss

rēs, reī, *f.*, wealth, thing, circumstance, affair, legal matter

resonō, resonāre, resonāvī, resound, echo

respectō, respectāre, wait for, keep on looking around or back at

respergō, respergere, respersī, respersum, sprinkle, sprinkle with stains

respondeō, respondēre, respondī, responsum, answer, reply; technical sense, appear in court

restituō, restituere, restituī, restitūtum, restore, revive

retineō, retinēre, retinuī, retentum, retain, keep, stop

retrahō, retrahere, retraxī, retractum, withdraw, draw back

revocō, revocāre, revocāvī, revocātum, recall, call back, restrain

rex, rēgis, *m.*, king

Rhēnus, -ī, *m.*, the river Rhine, considered the boundary between Gaul and Germany

Rhodus, -ī, *f.*, Rhodes, island off the coast of Lycia

Rhoetēus, -a, -um, *adj.*, of Rhoeteum, poetic word for Troy

rīdeō, rīdēre, rīdī, rīsum, laugh, laugh at

rixa, -ae, *f.*, fight

rōbur, rōboris, *n.*, oak tree, hard timber, strength

rogō, rogāre, rogāvī, rogātum, ask, ask for, ask a person to do something, make erotic overtures to, beg

Rōma, -ae, *f.*, Rome

Rōmulus, -ī, *m.*, Romulus, legendary founder of Rome

rubeō, rubēre, to become red

ruber, rubra, rubrum, *adj.*, red

rubor, rubōris, *m.*, redness, blush

rudens, rudentis, *m.*, ship's rope, rope

Rūfus, -ī, *m.*, Roman cognomen; may be the Marcus Caelius Rufus who had an affair with Clodia Metelli and whom Cicero defended successfully in his speech, the *Pro Caelio*

rūmor, rūmōris, *m.*, clamor, gossip, rumor, unfavorable report, favorable report

rumpō, rumpere, rūpī, ruptum, break, shatter, destroy

rūpēs, rūpis, *f.*, steep rocky cliff, crag

rursus, *adv.*, back, again, once again, on the other hand

rūs, rūris, *n.*, the country (as opposed to the town), farm, estate

S

Sabīnus, -a, -um, *adj.*, Sabine; the Sabines were a people of central Italy.

sacculus, -ī, *m.*, small bag; small bag used for holding money

sacer, sacra, sacrum, *adj.*, sacred, holy, detestable (as term of abuse, from the idea of "offensive to divine law")

saec(u)lum, -ī, *n.*, generation, age, lifetime, century

saepe, *adv.*, often

Saetabus, -a, -um, *adj.*, Saetaban, of or made in Saetabis, a town in Hispania Tarraconensis known for its linen

saevus, -a, -um, *adj.*, cruel, savage

Sagae, Sagārum, *m. pl.*, a Scythian people living on the northern borders of Persia.

sagittifer, sagittifera, sagittiferum, *adj.*, carrying arrows

sāl, salis, *m.*, salt, wit

salsus, -a, -um, *adj.*, salted, witty, funny

salūs, salūtis, *f.*, safety, health, salvation

salvē, singular imperative; hello, hail

sanctus, -a, -um, *adj.*, sacred, holy

sānē, *adv.*, soundly, really, truly, sesibly; *with adv. or adj.*, very, quite

sanguis, sanguinis, *m.*, blood

sapiō, sapere, sapīvī, have taste, be wise

Sapphicus, -a, -um, *adj.*, Sapphic, of Sappho, the Greek poet who wrote and lived on the island of Lesbos towards the end of the 7ᵗʰ century BCE

satiō, satiāre, satiāvī, satiātum, satisfy, sate, gratify

satis, *adv.*, enough, sufficiently; *indecl. noun*, enough

Sāturnālia, -ium, *n. pl.*, December 17 and following days of holiday, festival of Saturn, a time of merriment and freedom from restraint

saturō, saturāre, saturāvī, saturātum, satisfy, sate, saturate

Satyrus, -ī, *m.*, Satyr; demi-god of wild places, especially forests, having the form of a man with some animal characteristics

saucius, -a, -um, *adj.*, wounded

saxeus, -a, -um, *adj.*, made of stone, rocky, stony, unfeeling

scelestus, -a, -um, *adj.*, wicked, guilty of evil or criminal actions; used colloquially as term of abuse

scīlicet, *adv.*, evidently, of course, surely

sciō, scīre, scīvī, scītum, know

scītus, -a, -um, *adj.*, expert, clever

scopulus, -ī, *m.*, projecting rock, boulder

scortillum, -ī, *n.*, little prostitute, young prostitute, little/young tart

scrībō, scrībere, scripsī, scriptum, write

scrīnium, scrīnī, *n.*, case or shelf for holding letters or papyrus rolls in a bookstore or library; holder for other things

scriptor, scriptōris, *m.*, writer, scribe

scriptum, -ī, *n.*, writing, literary work (*usually in pl.*)

scurra, -ae, *m.*, fashionable idler, witty person

Scylla, -ae, *f.*, Scylla, half-human sea monster, located at the Straits of Messina, who grabbed and ate men from passing ships

sēcēdō, sēcēdere, sēcessī, sēcessum, withdraw

sector, sectārī, sectātus sum, pursue, chase

secundus, -a, -um, *adj.*, following, second, favorable

sed, *conj.*, but

sedeō, sedēre, sēdī, sessum, sit

sēdēs, sēdis, *f.*, seat, site, home, dwelling

semel, *adv.*, once, once and for all

sēmimortuus, -a, -um, *adj.*, half dead

semper, *adv.*, always

senecta, -ae, *f.*, old age

seneō, senēre, be old

senex, senis, *m.*, old man

sensus, sensūs, *m.*, any of the five physical senses, ability to perceive or make judgments, consciousness, feeling, sense

sentiō, sentīre, sensī, sensum, feel, sense, perceive, think, understand

sepeliō, sepelīre, sepelīvī, sepultum, bury, overcome

septemgeminus, -a, -um, *adj.*, sevenfold

Septimillus, -ī, *m.*, diminutive of Septimius

Septimius, Septimī, *m.*, Septimius, man's name

sepulcrum, -ī, *n.*, tomb, grave

sequor, sequī, secūtus sum, follow

Serāpis, Serāpis/Serāpidis, *m.*, Serapis, Egyptian god

sermō, sermōnis, *m.*, speech, talk, conversation, dialogue, topic of conversation

serō, serere, sēvī, satum, sow, plant

serva, -ae, *f.*, slave (female)

serviō, servīre, servīvī, servītum, serve as a slave, wait on, be politically subject, devote oneself to

Sestiānus, -a, -um, *adj.*, Sestian, related to Publius Sestius, quaestor in 63 BCE and helper of Cicero against Catiline

Sestius, Sestī, *m.*, Sestius; cf. **Sestiānus, -a, -um**

seu, *conj.*, or if, **seu . . . seu**, whether . . . or

sevērus, -a, -um, *adj.*, strict, severe, serious

sēvocō, sēvocāre, sēvocāvī, sēvocātum, call away, draw aside, separate

sī, *conj.*, if

sībilus, -ī, *m.*, a sibilant sound, hissing or whistling sound

sīc, *adv.*, so, thus, in this way; that is so, yes

siccus, -a, -um, *adj.*, dry, sober

sīcut, *adv.*, just as, as

sīdus, sīderis, *n.*, star; sky *(pl.)*

signum, -ī, *n.*, sign, distinguishing mark, image, constellation, military standard

Sīlēnus, -ī, *m.*, Silenus; attendant of Bacchus usually depicted as old, drunk, and bestial

silēscō, silēscere, become silent, grow quiet

silva, -ae, *f.*, forest

simul, *conj.*, as soon as (also with **atque** or **ac**); *adv.*, at the same time, at the same time as, once, together

sincērē, *adv.*, truly, faithfully

sine, *prep. with abl.*, without

singulī, -ae, -a, *pl. adj.*, single, individual

singultus, -ūs, *m.*, sob

sinister, sinistra, sinistrum, *adj.*, left, adverse

sinistrā, *adv.*, on the left

sinō, sinere, sīvī, situm, leave alone, allow

sinus, sinūs *m.*, fold in a garment, curve, breast, embrace, gulf

sī quis, sī qua/sī quae, sī quid (= sīquis, etc.), *indef. pron. and adj.*, if anybody, if anything, if any

Sirmiō, Sirmiōnis, *f.*, promontory in Lacus Benacus (Lago di Garda)

sistō, sistere, stetī, statum, set up, place firmly, make firm

sīve, *conj.*, or if, **sīve...sīve**, whether...or

sodālis, sodālis, *m.*, companion, comrade

sōl, sōlis, *m.*, sun, a day (as determined by the rising of the sun)

sōlāciolum, -ī, *n.*, a little comfort, a little solace, a little consolation

soleō, solēre, solitus sum, be accustomed

sōlus, -a, -um, *adj.*, alone, lonely, deserted

solvō, solvere, solvī, solūtum, loosen, break up, set free, perform duly, fulfill (as in a vow or promise)

somnus, -ī, *m.*, sleep

sonitus, -ūs, *m.*, sound

sordidus, -a, -um, *adj.*, dirty, degrading, vulgar

sospes, sospitis, *adj.*, safe and sound, unhurt

spectō, spectāre, spectāvī, spectātum, look at, watch

spērō, spērāre, spērāvī, spērātum, hope, hope for, expect

spēs, speī, *f.*, hope

spīnōsus, -a, -um, *adj.*, thorny, spiny, difficult

sponsus, -ī, *m.*, betrothed husband

spūmō, spūmāre, spūmāvī, spūmātum, foam, froth

spūmōsus, -a, -um, *adj.*, foaming, frothy

stāgnum, -ī, *n.*, expanse of standing water, pool

statuō, statuere, statuī, statūtum, set, stand, establish, decide

sternuō, sternuere, sternuī, sneeze

stīpendium, stīpendī, *n.*, regular cash payment, permanent tax, offering

stō, stāre, stetī, statum, stand

strophium, strophī, *n.*, breastband

studiōsus -a, -um, *adj.*, attentive, diligent, eager, zealous

studium, studī, *n.*, enthusiasm, eagerness, pastime, study

suāvior, suāviārī, suāviātus sum, kiss

suāvis, -e, pleasant, pleasing to the senses

sub, *prep. with acc. or abl.*, under, below

subitō, *adv.*, suddenly, quickly

sublevō, sublevāre, sublevāvī, sublevātum, lift, support, encourage, lighten

subrēpō, subrēpere, subrepsī, subreptum, creep under, come on gradually

subter, *prep. with acc. or abl.*, under

subtīlis, -e, *adj.*, fine in texture, delicate

suburbānus, -a, -um, *adj.*, situated close to the city (usually Rome), characteristic of those living near the city

succipiō, succipere, succēpī, succeptum, take, receive, undertake

sūdārium, sūdārī, *n.*, piece of cloth carried around and used for wiping the face or as a napkin

sūdō, sūdāre, sūdāvī, sūdātum, sweat, be damp

Suffēnus, -ī, *m.*, Suffenus; otherwise unknown

suī, sibi, sē, sē, *third person reflex. pron.*, himself, herself, itself, themselves

Sulla, -ae, *m.*, Sulla; otherwise unknown

sum, esse, fuī, futūrus, be

summus, -a, -um, *adj.*, highest, topmost

sūmō, sūmere, sumpsī, sumptum, take, take on

sumptuōsus, -a, -um, *adj.*, expensive, costly, extravagant

super, *adv.*, above, beyond, more than enough

superbus, -a, -um, *adj.*, proud, arrogant

superō, superāre, superāvī, superātum, get beyond, surpass, overcome, be superior to

supersum, superesse, superfuī, remain, survive

supplex, supplicis, *adj.*, suppliant

supplicium, supplicī, *n.*, entreaty, punishment, atonement, thing offered to propitiate someone

suppōnō, suppōnere, supposuī, suppositum, put under, place under

suprēmus, -a, -um, *adj.*, final, last

sūra, -ae, *f.*, calf of the leg

surripiō, surripere, surripuī, surreptum, steal

suspendō, suspendere, suspendī, suspensum, hang up

suspicor, suspicārī suspicātus sum, guess, imagine, suspect

suspīrō, suspīrāre, suspīrāvī, suspīrātum, sigh, breathe out

sustollō, sustollere, sustulī, sublātum, raise on high, kidnap

suus, -a, -um, *third person reflex. adj.*, his, her, its, their (own)

Syria, -ae, *f.*, Syria, area between Asia Minor and Egypt, usually including Phoenicia and Palestine

Syrtis, Syrtis, *f.*, Syrtis (*especially pl.*), name of two areas of sandy flats on the coast between Carthage and Cyrene; whole desert region next to this coast

T

tabella, -ae, *f.*, flat piece of wood, tablet, picture, wooden writing tablet usually coated with wax

taberna, -ae, *f.*, wooden hut, inn, shop

taceō, tacēre, tacuī, tacitum, be silent

tacitus, -a, -um, *adj.*, silent

taeter, taetra, taetrum, *adj.*, foul, horrible, vile, monstrous

talentum, -ī, *n.*, a weight of silver used as a Greek unit of currency, talent

tālis, -e, *adj.*, of such a kind

tam, *adv.*, to such a degree, so

tamen, *adv.*, nevertheless

tandem, *adv.*, at last, finally

tangō, tangere, tetigī, tactum, touch

tantum, -ī, *n. pron.*, so much; *adverbial use of acc.*, to such an extent, only

tantus, -a, -um, *adj.*, so great, of such a size, of such great magnitude; *pl.*, so many

tardipēs, tardipedis, *adj.*, slow-footed, lame

taurus, -ī, *m.*, bull

Taurus, -ī, *m.*, Taurus, mountain range in south of Asia Minor

tectum, -ī, *n.*, roof, house, dwelling

tegmen, tegminis, *n.*, cover

tegō, tegere, texī, tectum, cover, guard, close the eyes (in sleep)

tellūs, tellūris, *f.*, land, earth, country, ground

tēlum, -ī, *n.*, spear, missile, weapon, shaft

tempestās, tempestātis, *f.*, period, season, time, weather, storm

templum, -ī, *n.*, sacred precinct, temple

temptō, temptāre, temptāvī, temptātum, try, attempt

tempus, temporis, *n.*, time, occasion, proper time, an age or particular period in history, danger

tenebrae, -ārum, *f. pl.*, darkness

tenebricōsus, -a, -um, *adj.*, dark

teneō, tenēre, tenuī, tentum, hold

tener, tenera, tenerum, *adj.*, tender, delicate, soft, young

tenuis, tenue, *adj.*, slender, thin, slight, subtle

tepefaciō, tepefacere, tepefēcī, tepefactum, warm, make fairly hot

tepor, tepōris, *m.*, mild heat, warmth

teres, teretis, *adj.*, rounded, smooth, polished

tergum, -ī, *n.*, back

terra, -ae, *f.*, earth, land

Thēseus, Thēseī/Thēseos, *m.*, Theseus, son of Aegeus, king of Athens, (or of Poseidon in another version) and Aethra, daughter of Pittheus, king of Troezen

thiasus, -ī, *m.*, group devoted to cult of Bacchus, orgiastic dance, especially in honor of Bacchus

Thrācias, Thrāciae, *f.*, wind from west of north

Thunia, -ae, *f.*, Bithynia; an area, later a Roman province, on the northwest coast of Asia Minor

Tīburs, Tīburtis, *adj.*, of or belonging to Tibur, modern Tivoli, a town not far from Rome

timor, timōris, *m.*, fear

tintinō, tintināre, make a ringing sound

tollō, tollere, sustulī, sublātum, lift, raise, extol, take away, destroy

torpeō, torpēre, be physically numb, lack sensation

torpor, torpōris, *m.*, numbness, paralysis, unconsciousness, lethargy, drowsiness

torreō, torrēre, toruī, tostum, scorch, parch, burn

tot, *indecl. adj.*, so many

tōtus, -a, -um, *adj.*, the whole of, all

trabs, trabis, *f.*, beam of wood, trunk of tree, ship; by METONYMY, phallus

trādō, trādere, trādidī, trāditum, hand over, deliver, introduce

trans, *prep. with acc.*, across

trecentī, -ae, -a, *pl. adj.*, three hundred, used to denote a large number

tremulus, -a, -um, *adj.*, trembling, shaky, quivering

trēs, tria, *adj.*, three

tribuō, tribuere, tribuī, tribūtum, allot, assign, grant, bestow

tristis, -e, *adj.*, sad

Trōius, -a, -um, *adj.*, Trojan

truculentus, -a, -um, *adj.*, ferocious, aggressive

trux, trucis, *adj.*, harsh, savage

tū, tuī, tibi, tē, tē, *pron.*, you (*sing.*)

tueor, tuērī, tuitus sum, look at, watch over, protect

tum, *adv.*, then

tumulō, tumulāre, tumulāvī, tumulātum, cover with a burial mound

tunc, *adv.*, then

tundō, tundere, tutudī, tunsum, strike with repeated blows, beat

turbō, turbinis, *m.*, object that spins, whirlwind

turgidulus, -a, -um, *adj.*, swollen

turpis, -e, *adj.*, ugly, shameful, disgraceful

tussis, tussis, *f.*, cough

tūtus, -a, -um, *adj.*, safe, secure

tuus, -a, -um, *adj.*, your (*sing.*)

U

ūber, ūberis, *adj.*, rich, abundant

ubi, *rel. adv.*, where, when; *interr. adv.*, where

ūdus, -a, -um, *adj.*, wet, pliant

ulciscor, ulciscī, ultus sum, take revenge on, avenge

ullus, -a, -um, *adj.*, any

ultimus, -a, -um, *adj.*, last, farthest, extreme, earliest

ultrō, *adv.*, of one's own accord

umbilīcus, -ī, *m.*, navel, umbilical cord, cylinder or roller or stick on which papyrus roll was wound; *pl.*, when referring to one book, the ornamental knobs or bosses at the ends of roller projecting from the roll

umbra, -ae, *f.*, shade, shadow, ghost

umquam, *adv.*, ever

ūnā, *adv.*, together, at the same time

ūnanimus, -a, -um, *adj.*, sharing a single attitude, acting in accord

unctus, -a, -um, *adj.*, oiled, enriched

unda, -ae, *f.*, wave, water

unde, *interr. and rel. adv.*, from where, from whom, from which

undique, *adv.*, on all sides, everywhere

unguentum, -ī, *n.*, ointment, perfume

ūnicus, -a, -um, sole, one and only

ūnus, -a, -um, *adj.*, one, alone, sole

urbānus, -a, -um, *adj.*, of the city, urbane, sophisticated

urbs, urbis, *f.*, city; the city of Rome

Ūriī, -ōrum, *m. pl.*, name of some place associated with the cult of Venus, perhaps the same as Urium, a town on the Apulian coast of Italy

ūrō, ūrere, ussī, ustum, burn; *in pass.*, be on fire

urtīca, -ae, *f.*, stinging nettle (coarse herb with stinging hairs)

usque, *adv.*, continuously, continually, all the way

ustulō, ustulāre, ustulāvī, ustulātum, burn partially, scorch

ut, *conj. with indic.*, as, like, when, considering how, where; *with subj.*, so that, that, to; *interr. adv.*, how

uterque, utraque, utrumque, *adj., pron.*, each of two

utinam, *particle*, used to reinforce a wish expressed by subjunctive, "would that . . ."

ūtor, ūtī, ūsus sum, (with abl.), use, enjoy

utpote, *particle reinforcing explanatory clause*, naturally

utrum, *particle*, whether

V

vacuus, -a, -um, *adj.*, empty, free, available

vadum -ī, *n.*, shallow water, bottom of sea, waters of sea (*usually in pl.*)

vae, *interj.*, alas, alas for, woe to, bad luck to

vagor, vagārī, vagātus sum, wander

vagus, -a, -um, *adj.*, roaming, wandering

valdē, *adv.*, powerfully, greatly, extremely

valeō, valēre, valuī, valitum, be powerful, be strong enough to, be well, prevail; **valē** etc., goodbye, farewell

vallēs, vallis, *f.*, valley

vānescō, vānescere, vanish, become useless

vānus, -a, -um, *adj.*, empty, groundless, imaginary

variē, *adv.*, in different ways, variously

variō, variāre, variāvī, variātum, adorn with contrasting colors, variegate

varius, -a, -um, *adj.*, varied, of many different kinds

Vārus, -ī, *m.*, Alfenus Varus, jurist who became consul suffect in 39 BCE or Quintilius Varus, friend of Vergil and Horace, mourned by Horace in *Odes* 1.24

vastus, -a, -um, *adj.*, desolate, huge

Vatīniānus, -a, -um, of Vatinius; Publius Vatinius, prosecuted in 54 BCE by Calvus for illegal electioneering, defended successfully by Cicero

-ve, *conj.*, or

vēcors, vēcordis, *adj.*, mad, demented

vehō, vehere, vexī, vectum, carry; *passive in middle sense*, travel, sail

vel, *conj.*, or

vēlō, vēlāre, vēlāvī, vēlātum, cover, clothe

vēlum, -ī, *n.*, sail

velut, *adv.*, as, just as

vēmens, vēmentis, *adj.*, violent, powerful

venēnum, -ī, *n.*, poison, magical or medicinal potion

veniō, venīre, vēnī, ventum, come

vēnor, vēnārī, vēnātus sum, hunt

venter, ventris, *m.*, belly, abdomen, stomach

ventitō, ventitāre, ventitāvī, ventitātum, come frequently

ventōsus, -a, -um, *adj.*, windy, volatile

ventus, -ī, *m.*, wind

venus, veneris, *f.*, Venus, Roman goddess of love; love, charm, sexual activity; best throw at dice

venustās, venustātis, *f.*, charm, grace, attraction

venustē, *adv.*, in a charming or attractive manner

venustus, -a, -um, *adj.*, attractive, charming

vēr, vēris, *n.*, spring

Vērāniolus, -ī, *m.*, diminutive of Veranius

Vērānius, Vērānī, *m.*, Veranius, friend of Catullus

verbum, -ī, *n.*, word, verb, saying, speech

vērē, *adv.*, really, truly

vernus, -a, -um, occurring in spring, vernal

vērō, *adv., particle*, truly, indeed

Vērōna, -ae, *f.*, town in Transpadane Gaul, birthplace of Catullus.

versiculus, -ī, *m.*, brief line of verse; *(pl.)* light poetry

versō, versāre, versāvī, versātum, spin, turn, keep turning around; *pass. or reflex.*, keep going around, toss, writhe

versus, -ūs, *m.*, line of verse

vertex, verticis, *m.*, head, summit

vērum, *adv.*, but

vērus, -a, -um, *adj.*, true, real

vēsānus, -a, -um, *adj.*, acting without reason, mad

vester, vestra, vestrum, *adj.*, your *(pl.)*

vestigium, vestigī, *n.*, footprint, sole, track, vestige

vestis, vestis, *f.*, clothes, dress, cloth in form of covering or hanging

vetus, veteris, *adj.*, old, ancient

vexō, vexāre, vexāvī, vexātum, disturb, trouble, agitate, ravage

via, -ae, *f.*, road, street, way

vibrō, vibrāre, vibrāvī, vibrātum, wave, brandish, propel (a weapon) suddenly

vicis *(gen.)* *f.*, turn, situation, lot

videō, vidēre, vīdī, vīsum, see, understand; in passive, seem, appear

vigeō, vigēre, viguī, flourish, thrive

vigescō, vigescere, grow lively, gain strength

vīlis, -e, *adj.*, cheap, worthless

villa, -ae, *f.*, country-house, estate, farm

vinciō, vincīre, vinxī, vinctum, bind, encircle

vindex, vindicis, *m., f.*, avenger; here, as *adj.*, avenging

vīnum, -ī, *n.*, wine

violō, violāre, violāvī, violātum, violate, dishonor

vir, -ī, *m.*, man, husband

virgō, virginis, *f.*, girl of marriageable age, young woman, virgin, maiden

virtūs, virtūtis, *f.*, manhood, courage, valor, virtue

vīsō, vīsere, vīsī, look at, go and see

vīta, -ae, *f.*, life; HYPERBOLICALLY, of a person as a term of affection

vīvō, vīvere, vixī, victum, live

vix, *adv.*, hardly, scarcely, just

vocō, vocāre, vocāvī, vocātum, call, summon, invite

volitō, volitāre, volitāvī, volitātum, fly, move about rapidly

volō, velle, voluī, wish, want, be willing

volō, volāre, volāvī, volātum, fly, speed

voluntās, voluntātis, *f.*, will, wish, intention

voluptās, voluptātis, *f.*, pleasure, delight

Volusius, Volusī, *m.*, Volusius, otherwise unknown

volvō, volvere, volvī, volūtum, roll, turn over (in the mind)

vorō, vorāre, vorāvī, vorātum, devour

vōs, vestrī/vestrum, vōbīs, vōs, vōbīs, *pron.*, you *(pl.)*

vōtum, -ī, *n.*, vow, prayer, votive offering

voveō, vovēre, vōvī, vōtum, promise (to a god) in return for a favor, vow, pray or long for

vox, vōcis, *f.*, voice, sound, words

vulgus, -ī, *n.*, the common people, the general public, crowd

vultus, -ūs, *m.*, look, face

Z

zephyrus, -ī, *m.*, west wind, Zephyr

zōna, -ae, *f.*, belt, girdle